Norse Mythology

Fascinating Myths and Legends of Norse Gods, Heroes, and Viking Beliefs

Table of Contents

Introduction..1

Chapter 1: In the Beginning 15

    Before the Beginning and After 16

    Yggdrasil and the Nine Worlds 20

    Mimir's Head and Odin's Eye 23

    Thor and His Undead Goats 25

Chapter 2: Norse Gods and Goddesses 26

    The Aesir and Vanir 27

    The Treasures of the Gods......................................30

    Loki and the Master Builder 31

    Freyja's Unusual Wedding 33

    The Norns 34

Chapter 3: The Children of the Gods............................36

    Thor and Baldr 36

    The Children of Loki 38

    The Domain of Hel 41

    The Death of Baldr 42

Chapter 4: Heroes and Sagas 47

    Overview of Sagas...50

    Heroes Mentioned in Sagas.....................................52

    The Mead of Poets 54

    The Birth of Sigurd 55

    Regin and Sigurd 57

    The Volsunga Saga and the Nibelungenlied 59

Chapter 5: Tales of Odin.............................. 61

Odin the Host and Odin the Guest 61

Geirroed and Odin.. 63

Chapter 6: Tales of Thor 65

Thor and Geirrod 66

Thor's Journey to the Land of the Giants............................. 67

Hymir and Thor's Finishing Expedition 69

Chapter 7: Tales of Loki 72

The Kidnapping of Idun... 72

The Last Day of Loki 75

Chapter 8: Lighter Tales of Norse Characters........... 77

The Marriage of Njord and Skadi.. 77

The Apples of Immortality 79

The Story of Gerd and Freyr.. 79

Chapter 9: Ragnarok.................................... 81

The Final Destiny of the Gods 81

Chapter 10: Twenty Little Known Facts about Norse Mythology and Viking Beliefs 83

Fact One: The Gods, Heroes, and Other Characters of Norse Myth and Legend Were Attested in Documents in the Old Norse Languages, the Progenitor of the Modern Languages of Scandinavia. 83

Fact Two: Most of the Old Norse Texts That Still Exist Today Come from Iceland... 84

Fact Three: Many Norse Legends Involve People Who Actually Lived and Were Not Merely the Stuff of Myth and Legend. 84

Fact Four: The Prose Edda and Poetic Edda Are Two Important Works from the Thirteenth Century That Serve as Invaluable Sources of Information About Norse Myth and the Time of the Vikings.......................... 85

Fact Five: The Norse Personified Many Things in Their Cosmology as Gods or Humanlike Beings. 85

Fact Six: The Norse Divided Their Gods into Two Main Groups: The Aesir and the Vanir. 86

Fact Seven: The Norse Believed in Many Types of Beings Besides the Gods, Including the Giants, Elves, Dwarfs, Famous Horses, Monsters, and Others. 86

Fact Eight: The Giants, or Jotunn, Were Particularly Important in Norse Mythology. They Even Sired Children by the Gods of the Aesir, Including Loki and Thor. 87

Fact Nine: According to Attestations from the Norse Period, the Giants Were Formed Before the Gods. 87

Fact Ten: The Famous Trickster God Loki Was Actually a Giant, Though He Was Admitted into the Aesir Group of Gods. 88

Fact Eleven: Thor Is Perhaps the Most Famous of the Norse Gods Because of His Mention in Media, Such as Film, Cartoons, and Comic Books. 88

Fact Twelve: Although Attestations Are Not Particularly Clear on the Nine Worlds That Flank Yggdrasil, Today These Worlds Have Been Granted Specific Identities Based on Information from the Norse Period. 89

Fact Thirteen: Odin Was the All-Father in Norse Myth: The Most Important Member of the Pantheon of Gods and Goddesses. 90

Fact Fourteen: The Valkyries May Have Been Peripheral Figures in Most Norse Stories, but They Have Become One of the More Popular Subjects for Artists and Writers in the Modern Period. 90

Fact Fifteen: Norse Paganism or Odinism Has Experienced a Revival in Many Areas, Including Iceland. 91

Fact Sixteen: Frigg Was the Wife of Odin. She Was Believed to Know the Destiny of All Things, but Never Reveals Her Knowledge. 91

Fact Seventeen: The Dead Could Go to Several Different Places. They Could Go to the Domain of Hel, Beneath Niflheim. They Could Be Chosen by the Valkyries and taken to Valhalla. or They Could Be Selected by Freyja to Dwell with Her in Her Land of Folkvangr. 92

Fact Eighteen: Much of the Fame of Norse Myth Comes from the 19th Century When Works by Men like the Grimm Brothers and William Wagner Became Popular. 92

Fact Nineteen: Most Norse Myths Were Actually Written down in the Christian Period, After the Practice of Worshipping the Norse Gods Had Actually Disappeared. 93

Fact Twenty: In English, Tuesday Is a Day of the Week That Originates from the Old Norse Language and Belief System. 94

Chapter 11: List of Norse Gods and Goddesses 95
Frequently Asked Questions 102
Conclusion 120

Introduction

Norse Mythology: Fascinating Myths and Legends of Norse Gods, Heroes, and Viking Beliefs explores the legends and belief system of a people who flourished more than one thousand years ago. The Norse may not have left much in the way of architecture, but they did leave other things. They left a great deal of runestones littered across the landscape; they left descendants in many of the areas they conquered, such as England and Normandy (in France); and they left a terrible memory in the fear that they inspired in those they fought against. This legacy is well attested in the records of the Vikings who terrorized the coasts of Europe for centuries. In this book, you will learn about some of the hundreds of characters from this highly singular mythology, one of the unique mythologies of the world.

Norse myths and legends have long sustained the imagination of millions around the world. Indeed, Norse Gods and heroes have permeated into mainstream culture in the form of popular characters from films and television shows to even the English names for days of the week. Norse myth has become a part of us in ways that we can only begin to imagine. Indeed, the Norse God Thor embodies too many in the Western world the ideal of strength and masculinity while the trickster God Loki represents some of the more sinister and unpredictable elements of Man.

But the world of Norse myth was very different from our own, as you will soon learn. The people at the heart of Norse civilization - living in modern-day Scandinavia, Northern Germany, as well as other areas of Norse settlement like Iceland and the British Isles - these people were part of a culture so far removed from how we think and perceive today as to be almost unrecognizable. In fact, in a well-known Scandinavian movie from the 1970s, a Viking character speaks disparagingly of the Christian Europeans to the South with their God nailed to a cross. Their society was so different from that of the Christians they pillaged as to render the Christians unfathomable.

Indeed, the Viking way of life has left an indelible mark on Europe. Though the cities that they pillaged were rebuilt long ago, and the people that they made into thralls, or slaves, have long since died, the Viking memory seems to persist right on to the present. Indeed, with the possible exception of the Mongols, there are few groups in history the mere mention of which strikes fear in the hearts of men. The Vikings truly were a people set apart.

This is the image that most people have of the practitioners of Norse myth: the Vikings. The term Viking really refers to the men and women who left their Scandinavian homeland to go pillaging, but the term has entered colloquial usage to refer to all of the people who formed part of Norse civilization. In this book, we will refer to Norse people and Germanic people in order to refer to the speakers of particular languages and language families. Many of the myths and characters described here first had their stories written down in medieval times when Christianity made written language (not to mention peaceful living) slightly more common than it had been in prior years. This allowed writers from these areas to put to paper what would have previously formed part of oral tradition.

The point, of course, is to spend a moment speaking about language. The men and women who followed Norse beliefs spoke a language referred to today as Old Norse. This language is the ancestor of the modern languages of Danish, Norwegian, Swedish, and Icelandic (as well as some other local languages). Old Norse was a Germanic language, which means it belongs to the Germanic branch of the Indo-European language family. In spite of this, Old Norse (and even modern Scandinavian languages) have some features that render them quite distinct from other members of the Indo-European language family. For one thing, there are several letters in Old Norse that are retained in languages like Icelandic or Swedish, but are absent from modern related languages like German and English.

In this book, most names of characters and Gods are written in Old Norse. In the case of names where one or more letters are non-existent in English, the names are written with the equivalent (phonetic) letters in English. In some cases, the names of Gods and other characters are written in languages where the name may be more common, such as Old English or Old Germanic. This represents the reality that some characters managed to enter the myths and histories of areas of Norse settlement or pillaging. Or, in the case of Siegfried and the Nibelungenlied, the German version of the story is simply more well-known than the Norse version.

This is a good stage to mention that Norse myth overlaps in a fair measure with the beliefs of the wider world of the Germanic peoples. The Norse themselves were a Germanic people who lived on the Jutland peninsula (most of which is modern Denmark) and the Scandinavian peninsula. From there they ventured to other areas like the Faroe Islands, Iceland, Greenland, Normandy, and the British Isles. Because of this overlap with the Germanic world, many characters from Norse mythology have a presence in modern Germanic culture. Of course, the most obvious example of this is the tale of Sigurd (or Sigurdr in Old Norse) whom the Germans knew as Siegfried. Sigurd or Siegfried was the center of several important tales, of which the most important today is that of the Nibelungenlied because of the cycle of operas that William Wagner composed on this subject.

But Sigurd was the center of other tales, too. The Nibelungenlied is the name of a poem written in modern-day Bavaria in the early 13th century. The poem is believed to have been based on tales that had been transmitted orally for at least several centuries before that when most of the Germanic world would have been pagan. It is easy to forget this pagan history of Europe, but it is very important to understand the sort of world that the people who believed in these myths and heroes came from. They did not live in a world of heaven and hell, but in a realm of Niflheim and Muspellsheim.

But back to Sigurd. Sigurd, or Siegfried, was a part of what would be described today as Norse myth and legend, as opposed to Germanic myth and legend. That the distinction between the two is more academic than anything else will be touched on at several junctures in this book. Sigurd appears in three of the seminal works of Norse mythology: The *Poetic Edda*, the *Prose Edda*, and the *Volsunga Saga*. Like most Norse myths touched on in this book, the great feats and exploits of Sigurd would have been recited by skalds and others. Poems and other myths were also recorded on runestones. Indeed, the earliest documented mention of Sigurd occurs in runestones from Sweden.

Skalds would have played an important role in the transmission of Norse myth, a role that had parallels throughout the Indo-European culture of Europe before the modern period. Skalds, bards, and poets of a similar type existed across the continent, transmitting stories of legendary figures as well as the exploits of men and women who had actually lived. Some scholars suggest that some of the Norse Gods, including Thor, may have originated from historical figures who were transformed into Gods because of the manner in which their stories were told and the duration of the telling.

In the case of Sigurd or Siegfried, it has been argued that he was a king from the Frankish dynasty of the Merovingians. The

Franks were a Germanic tribe who settled in the region of modern-day France at the end of the Roman period. This German tribe gave their name to the nation of France though they adopted the Latin language of the people they subjugated as well as other accouterments of Latin culture. The tale of Sigurd as told in most of these works center on his slaying of the dragon Fafnir and his relationship with Brunhild and his wife Gudrun. The tales of Sigurd will be discussed in the fourth and eighth chapters. The importance of sagas and other source texts will be discussed further in the fourth chapter.

The distinction between Norse and Germanic society seems real to us today, but likely would have been unusual to people living at the time. The real distinction lay between Christians and non-Christians, as the Norse were. It is interesting to ponder that most of the Norse myths that have been passed down to us originate from people who were Christians at the time they wrote these poems and told these sagas. Even the runestones of Sweden, upon which many poems and legends are inscribed, often date from the Christian period.

Norse Mythology: Fascinating Myths and Legends of Norse Gods, Heroes, and Viking Beliefs explores the legends of Norse mythology in the context of the various stories. This parallels the manner in which these myths were told: as heroic legends of gods and men as told by poet and skald. This review of Norse mythology, therefore, involves a submersion in the manner in which Norse stories were transmitted to the Norse people who were their audience. These stories were told by poets and skalds who enthralled their audience of jarl, freeman, and thrall with the tales of men who might have lived once but eventually came to walk the halls of the Gods.

In the first chapter, an introduction to Norse myth is undertaken through an examination of the beginnings of the Norse Gods and heroes. The earliest tales start with the very beginning: the abyss that is the universe bound on either side by worlds of ice and fire. It was from this world that Gods, giants, and the earliest men emerged. This chapter will involve the tales that encompass the start of Norse myth. The reader will learn about Yggdrasil and the Nine Worlds. The Nine Worlds remain a subject of some mystery, but it is an interesting subject nonetheless. The reader will also discover the tale of the giant Mimir's Head and Odin's eye. It was through Mimir that Odin gained his wisdom.

The Gods and Goddesses of the Norse world are the center of many myths and legends from this long-gone society. Like the Greeks and many other cultures whose pantheon of Gods is known to us, the speakers of the Old Norse tongue saw their world as beginning with Gods and giants. Men came later, created by Gods who were bored or merely fashioned them without any particular purpose. Like the Greeks, the world of the Norse people was also inhabited by many others, including dwarfs, elves, dragons, monsters, and all of the other races and creatures that make legends interesting and easily recalled by someone who might have heard them as a child: all those years ago.

There were many Gods and Goddesses in the Norse pantheon, so many that the last chapter is devoted to a list of the major characters. This chapter is intended for use as a reference. If the reader chooses, they can consult this chapter to jog their memory about this person or that, or to get a sense of how one important character is related to another. Norse mythology is remarkable for the propensity to name things, such as the children of Gods or heroes, even if these characters never appear again. Even things like wells, horses, weapons, helmets and such are all given specific (and sometimes very long) names. Let us not forget the all the strange places in the Norse world also were name.

Norse mythology has specific concepts about God. Among the Gods, there were the Aesir and Vanir: the new Gods as well as the old ones. There were tales about the treasures of the Gods. Of course, there was the ring of the Nibelung, fashioned by a dwarf. In the second chapter, in addition to an introduction to the deities of Norse myth, the reader will also be exposed to some of the formative stories that fall under this scope, including the tale of Loki and the Master Builder, which comes from the Prose Edda, and the tale of Freyja's Unusual Wedding, a wedding which really did not involve Freyja at all.

Gods can beget other Gods as well as heroes. In this respect, Norse mythos was, again, not unlike that of the Greeks. The Greeks saw the line between Gods and men as being very real, but this line was inhabited by demigod's - Godlike heroes who challenged the Gods themselves - nymphs, monsters, and others who seemed to wander into the realm of the immortal rather than to dwell in the halls of men like the common folk of the Greek world. Indeed, heroes were important in Greek myth because they represented to some degree the role played by the listener, that ordinary person who has to understand what place they play in a time where the Gods were whimsical and cruel.

Though we know so much more about what the Greeks thought (and how they thought), this sort of purpose for mythology must also have been true of the people of the Norse world. The world they lived in was stratified, too, and it must have been important for the jarl to know how he was different from the Gods, just as it was important for the ordinary man to know he was different from the jarl (or from the thrall at the other end of the spectrum). Indeed, the Norse even had a God whom they believed to be responsible for social stratification. In chapter three, we will hear tales about the children of the Gods, those men and women who often occupied the liminal ground between heaven and earth.

A tale of the children of the Gods - of Thor and Baldr, and of the children of Loki - naturally leads into a tale of heroes. An exploration of the heroes of Norse legend requires an understanding of how their tales were recorded. These tales were recorded in the form of poems and sagas. Saga is the name for the heroic literature that pertains to the Gods and heroes of Norse myth. As stated previously, some of the figures of these tales may have been real men who lived and became mythical. As also stated, many of these sagas were written in the 12th and 13th centuries, when the Norse had been Christianized by the people, they had previously enslaved and carried off to far off places like Iceland and Greenland.

Although it sometimes is unclear whether the characters in Norse tales were real or fictional, sometimes the distinction is pretty clear. For instance, there is a type of saga called a Saga of Icelanders, which involves characters who played formative roles in the colonization of that place. Their legends generally begin in Norway and then take root in Iceland. Most of these sagas are regarded as historical, a fact which will be explored in the fourth chapter along with other related topics.

The story of the saga is also a tale of the storyteller. In the fourth chapter, an exploration of sagas and the writers of sagas will naturally lead to the tales of the heroes themselves. So many sagas have been left to us that it is nearly impossible to describe them in a portion of a single chapter. The reader will learn about some of the more important sagas, including *Egils saga* and the *Volsunga Saga*. The reader will also learn some of the tales of the heroes, such as the story of Sigurd and Regin (in addition to some of the other tales about Sigurd).

The individual Gods of Norse myth had many tales onto themselves. There were tales about Odin, Loki, Thor, Freyja, Freyr, Baldr, as well as many others: enough to fill several volumes. Starting with the fifth chapter, some of the tales of the major figures of Norse mythology will be explored, beginning with Odin, the father of the Gods. Odin was akin to Zeus in Greek myth or Jupiter in Roman myth. He was Odin All-Father - the kingly and fatherly figure of Norse myth - although he was a sometimes-mischievous figure in the Norse tradition, which was not necessarily the same as how other cultures viewed the twin role of father and king.

Thor is one of the central figures of Norse myth though the reasons may come as a surprise. Thor, like Heracles in Greek myth or Hercules in Roman myth, was essentially the idealized male figure. He embodied male strength and power, twin ideals that were themselves encapsulated in the form of Thor's infamous hammer, Mjolnir. Thor, therefore, was an important figure in Norse mythos because of the figure he cut as a representative of the Norse idea of maleness, but much of Thor's importance actually dates to modern times.

Thor is also the name of a popular comic book character, based on the original hero of Norse and Germanic myth. Thor has grown to be a common figure in modern culture because of the movies that have been made about the comic book character, not to mention the other fictional portrayals in literature that ultimately derive from myth. It, therefore, becomes important to distinguish the Norse idea of Thor from the modern one. In the sixth chapter, the reader will learn tales of Thor to help form an idea of the original character. Tales of Thor and Geirrod, Thor's journey to the Land of the Giants, and Hymir and Thor's expedition will all be related.

Loki is perhaps the most interesting of the major figures of Norse legend. Many groups had a trickster or villainous figure in their myths: a role occupied very adeptly by the Norse God, Loki. But Loki is a little different from the occasional mischievous figures in other mythological traditions. Loki was not the enemy of the Gods for most of Norse legend. Indeed, Loki was ranked among the Aesir - the chief Gods of Norse myth - though he technically was a giant as he was born to a giant and a giantess. The giants are almost universally characterized as malign in Norse myth, and the career of Loki would seem to justify this place.

Yet Loki was still counted among the Aesir, the leader of which was Odin, and this trickster God was often consulted by them. Indeed, the Gods frequently used Loki's adroitness in this area to their benefit. The idea of Loki seems almost to validate or to solemnize the role of trickery in society, seeming nearly to say that every culture has a need for a God-like this. Like the other Gods, Loki would have been prayed to and worshipped, though he may not have been as popular a figure as Odin or Thor. The Kidnapping of Idun is one of a couple of tales that will be told about the infamous Loki.

There are many tales of heroes and lesser figures that help to give a sense of how the Scandinavians of the time viewed their world and their own relationship to it. This is really the role that mythology plays: to answer the twin questions of who are we and why are we. And this is what Norse mythology does well: it gives us a sense of how the Norse were different from both the people that came before and the people that came after.

Indeed, much of the popularity of Norse mythology today has to do with the image that we have of the Vikings. Even one thousand years later, the devastation caused by the Vikings in their "going Viking" expeditions has served the role of propaganda, creating an image of strength, brutality, and near invincibility that makes the myths of these people somehow more compelling. Whether the Norse people as a whole were as Viking as modern storytelling purports them to be is another story entirely. Indeed, some of the stories left to us by travelers during the Viking period suggest that the people of this time were as remarkable for their poor standards of hygiene as they were for their exploits on the battlefield. Of course, lack of cleanliness does not generally sell movies about Thor, does it?

Some of the lighter tales that will be covered in the eighth chapter include the story of the apples of immortality, the marriage of Njord and Skaldi, and the story of Gerd and Frey (or Freyr in Old Norse). These are only lighter or lesser tales because the figures they describe are lesser-known, peripheral figures in Norse mythology to the general public of today. In fact, examination of some of these tales helps to examine the idea of a common origin of many ideologies in the myths of various peoples.

In the ninth chapter, the final destiny of the Gods will be explored as Ragnarok is examined. Ragnarok, the twilight of the

Gods, has become a word widely known today because of its use in film, though, like other terms from Norse myth, what it stood for represented more than what people familiar with it would think of today. Indeed, there is a lot about Norse mythology and Viking society that would come as a surprise to readers. In the tenth chapters, twenty facts about the myths and beliefs of Old Norse speakers will be examined to help the reader obtain a final idea about what it really meant to live in this time.

The world of the Norse may have been a long time ago, but if you travel to the fjords of Norway and the icy glaciers of Northern Scandinavia, Iceland, and Greenland it is easy to be transported back to this world. To the Norse, the world was not filled with worries about heaven and hell, but with real fears about inglorious defeat in battle or the wrath of the Gods. Understanding the myths of the Norse allows you to understand who the Vikings were, and who the hundreds of thousands of Norse who were not Vikings were. It all begins with a journey into their collective head: a scenic tour through the abyss that was the universe in its earliest days.

Chapter 1: In the Beginning

The Norse universe was formed out of blackness. It was out of this blackness, or abyss, that the earliest creatures were formed: the giants who rapidly spread in number, and the cow called Audhumla who was responsible for nurturing both giant and God alike. The various physical places of the universe were formed as these various creatures were formed, and it would soon come to be inhabited by not only God and giant, but good elves and dark elves, dwarfs, serpents, monsters, and men. In this chapter, we will learn about the Norse origin myths as well as be introduced to the Gods who formed the center of Norse mythos.

Most of what we know about Norse religion comes not from the practitioners of the religion itself, but from their descendants who had been Christianized. Indeed, much of our understanding of both early Norse history and Norse mythology comes from the sagas and poems writ in the 13th century and later. Many of these sagas were transcribed into volumes in the 18th and 19th centuries, allowing a new generation of readers to be exposed to a way of life that was very far removed from their own. In this Romantic period, Norse legend took on a fantasy quality, not unlike that which it would have had for its practitioners in the heyday of practice.

But to the speakers of Old Norse, the legends of Odin, Thor, Loki, and Freyja were not fantasying, but very real. These people sought to honor their Gods who were warlike and sometimes fickle by being valiant in war. Indeed, the image we have of the Vikings is of a people continuously in conflict. If their own lands were under the spell of a temporary peace, they rectified this situation by invading foreign lands. Indeed, these Viking invaders were not unlike the Viking Gods themselves, who were also quarrelsome and bellicose. Here we will begin to learn about these Gods and Goddesses, allowing us to also peek inside the minds of the people who attempted to emulate them.

At the center of the Norse pantheon was Odin. Odin was the grandson of Buri, who came into being when the cow Audhumla licked a boulder of salt. Buri was the father of Borr who fathered Odin. Odin had two brothers, Villi and Ve, and they were the progenitors of the race of Gods known as the Aesir. But the Aesir were not alone in being sprung from the universe. The giants, or jotun, also were nurtured by the cow Audhumla, but these giants sprung spontaneously. As the ice of Niflheim was heated by the fires of Muspellsheim, streams of venom poured out of Niflheim to form the giants. But more on this to come.

Before the Beginning and After

The early Gods and giants emerged from the great abyss. This profound abyss was called Ginnunga-gap, and it was confined on either side by two regions. On one side was Niflheim, the land of mists and ice. On the other side was Muspellsheim, or the Home of Desolation, which was a land of heat and fire. The melting of the ice of Niflheim led to the formation of the giants, or jotun, of which the first was called Ymir (or Aughelmir). Another living thing was also formed at this time, the cow Audhumla whose milk was used by Ymir for sustenance. The image of God and the giant being suckled by Audhumla became a popular image in Scandinavian painting in the 18th century and after. The other giants sprung from Ymir, and these giants were collectively regarded as an evil race. In this respect, Norse mythology draws parallels with Greek myth which features the Titans, the old Gods with whom the newer Olympian Gods struggled and eventually overthrew.

The Norse Gods, when they eventually arose, would, too, struggle with their predecessors. Where the Titans are somewhat ambiguous in their relative goodness or badness, the giants, or jotun, seem to be unequivocally bad in Norse myth. The giants, though they came first, definitely seem to be burdened with very bad PR. Unfortunately, this bad PR was present even in the Viking period. In this respect, the giants seem to be a synthesis of both the old Gods and monsters of other Indo-European mythologies.

As was touched upon in the previous section, Buri was the first God who was created when Audhumla licked a boulder of salt bound to ice. Buri had a son called Borr. Borr fathered with Bestla, who was a daughter of one of the giants (a certain Bolthorn), three sons. One of these sons was Odin, the All-Father of the Norse pantheon. The other brothers were called Villi and Ve. These three were the forefathers of the race of Gods known as the Aesir.

The sons of Borr eventually quarreled with the giants. According to Norse myth, the descendants of Ymir began to proliferate until they reached a great number. The sons of Borr – thus, Odin, Villi, and Ve – slew Ymir. Also dying in the tumult were all of the giants except for a certain Bergelmir. It was said that Bergelmir was saved by his wife by means of a seafaring vessel. The sons of Borr, including Odin, therefore failed to slay all of the giants, and the descendants of Berghelmir would eventually begin to proliferate, too, until they reached great numbers.

The Norse had several names for the giants who appeared in many sagas and poems. The giants – known in plural as jotun or in singular as jotunn – were also called ettins, cliff-ettins, thursar, rime-thursar, and trolls. Yes, this is the ultimate origin of the term troll in English. It was said that the sons of Borr created three portions of the world from the body of Ymir: that is, the earth, the sea, and the sky. It was the body of Ymir which formed the soil of the earth while the bones became mountain ranges, the skull became the roof of heaven, the hair became grass and trees, and the brain was formed into clouds. Even the maggots feasting within the body of Ymir were used to form something: in this case, the dwarfs who lived below the level of the earth. It was said that the dwarfs as a race were closer to the jotun than they were to the Aesir.

Odin, Villi, and Ve – the three sons of Borr – also created the bodies of the universe. The sun and moon were drawn by horses that, in typical Norse fashion, had been named. The horses that drew the sun were called Alvsin and Arvak. Two children of a certain Mundilfari were appointed to be the drivers of the two horses Alvsin and Arvak. These children were said to be otherworldly beautiful and they were named Sun and Moon after these respective bodies.

The universe was also peopled with other beings besides the giants (jotun) and the Gods (Aesir). We have already mentioned the dwarfs, created from the maggots that fed on the giant Ymir's body. There were also the elves and the Vanir. The Vanir were Gods that had the responsibility for directing nature. They lived in a place called Vanaheim. The Aesir quarreled with the Vanir, some of whom occupied similar roles to the powerful Vanir. War raged between the two groups of Gods until peace was affected by the agreement for both sides to exchange hostages. The Vanir sent Njord, who became one of the Aesir, while the Aesir sent Hoenir. These were not the only deities exchanged. Freyr and Freyja, who will be discussed later, also came originally from the Vanir.

The last major race to discuss is the race of the elves. It seems to be characteristically Norse (and Germanic) that these creatures are not wholly good or evil but can have both characteristics. Some elves were evil while others were good. The good elves dwelled in a place called Alfheim, which is also the name for a region in Norway, while the bad elves (or dark elves) dwelled below the Earth's surface. Because they dwelled here, the so-called dark elves are sometimes conflated with dwarfs.

This portion of Norse mythology would not be complete without a brief sojourn into the stories of Ragnarok: the Norse apocalypse. The descendants of the first humans – Ask and Embla – are wiped out in the great war between the Gods and the remaining descendants of Ymir. Great flames envelop the world, but this great cataclysm only sets the stage for the world to be reborn again, anew, in the same pattern of events that existed previously. This type of story, though singular and interesting, does hearken back to Eastern ideas of rebirth as found in religions like Hinduism. Ragnarok will be discussed further in a later chapter.

Yggdrasil and the Nine Worlds

Before we get to Yggdrasil, it is important to mention the land where the Gods dwelled. The sons of Borr were the first of the Aesir, but other Gods came later. The Aesir lived in Asgard, which was one of the Nine Worlds. According to the *Prose Edda* (specifically the *Gylfaginning*), Asgard was surrounded by a wall that had been erected by a giant (jotun) riding a horse. Odin and his wife Frigg had high places appointed to them in Asgard. Odin was associated with twelve other Gods of the Aesir in the hall known as Gladsheim while Frigg was associated with her peer Goddesses in a hall called Vingolf. There was also a hall called

Valaskjalf, which had a silver roof, but the most important hall of all was Valhalla.

Valhalla was the hall where the Gods of the Aesir had their banquets. This hall had doorways or portals through which honored warriors would march. After their deaths, such warriors were brought to Valhalla into the presence of Odin. It was said that there were portals 640 in number in Valhalla, and through each of these 960 brave heroes could march shoulder to shoulder. In addition to the grandeur of Valhalla, there was also Bifrost, a bridge that connected heaven and earth. The bridge is red like fire and it burns to keep the jotun from crossing it.

It has been mentioned that Odin was assisted by twelve Aesir, who were the chief Gods of the Norse religion. They had their counsels in Gladsheim, where they had high seats on pedestals assigned to them. These Gods were regarded as being governors of the universe. They had counsel among one another in Gladsheim, and their high seats in this place were regarded as seats of judgment. The Gods were believed to be mighty, victorious in war, and just. Justice seemed to be more important to the Norse than some other people's even though the sagas are rife with tales of injustice, some of which originated with the Gods themselves. It was believed that the Aesir were fond of the race of men, protecting them from jotun, dark elves, dwarfs, and others. In this regard, the Norse Gods perhaps were not as equivocal as the Olympian Gods of Greece and Rome.

Yggdrasil was the great tree of the universe that connected the Nine Worlds. Yggdrasil is believed today to have been an ash tree although the components of this name do not indicate a tree. Yggdrasil means Odin's horse in Old Norse, and there is some speculation that Yggdrasil was actually the tree that this horse was tethered to. In the Poetic Edda, also called the Older Edda, a tale is mentioned in which Odin hung himself from a tree and it is thought that Yggdrasil could be the gallows that Odin hung from. The name of Yggdrasil is further complicated by the term askr Yggdrassil, which specifically denotes an ash tree to which Odin's horse has been bound. The term could also refer to a yew tree.

The tales of Yggdrasil are closely tied to the earliest times, even before the Gods. Around Yggdrasil exist nine worlds. There are also nine wood-ogresses (nio idithiur). In a poem of the Poetic Edda, a shamanic woman (or volva) describes remembering the earliest times when the tree Yggrasil was merely a seed. Though the nine worlds of Yggdrasil may not be named, there is a proliferation of threes about the tree. There is a lake under the tree from which come three maidens steeped in knowledge. The tree Yggdrasil has three branches under which live Hel, frost giants, and under the last, mankind.

There were also a number of other important places and functions associated with Yggdrasil. The Gods of the Aesir resorted to this tree for their things, or assemblies. It has been mentioned that under one of the roots lived frost jotunn. This root was in the depths of Niflheim and here also lay a well called Vergelmir. In this well lived a terrible serpent called Nidhogg as well as many other serpents who gnawed at the roots day and night in an attempt to undermine and destroy the world tree Yggdrasil.

Near another one of the roots, there was another well where lived a wizened giant called Mimir, to whom the well belonged. This well was a font of wisdom, and Mimir drank from it each day. Besides jotun and serpents, many animals also made their home in this tree. Tales tell of a squirrel that was constantly ferrying communication from a sinister eagle to the serpent Nidhogg.

Yggdrasil appears again in the end times. As part of the beginning of Ragnarök, Gjallarhorn is blown by Heimdall, the God Odin talks with the head of Mimir, and Yggdrasil shivers and the giant breaks free.

Mimir's Head and Odin's Eye

The wisest of all of the Gods was Odin. Indeed, Odin has many names in Norse poems and sagas. He was the supreme, father deity in Norse mythology, akin to Zeus in Greek myth or Jupiter in Roman myth. As epithets are common in myths (including Norse myths), Odin went by many names. Besides the name of All-Father, as Odin was often called, this deity was also known as Valfather, or Father of the Slain; Gaut or Geat, The Creator; Bolverk, The Worker of Misfortune; Baleyg, The One with Flaming Eyes; Sigfather, The Father of Victory; Ygg, The Awful (also may indicate a yew tree); Har, The High One; Herjan, God of Battles; Gagnrad, The Determiner of Victories; Jafnhar, Even as High; Thridi: Third (a name inspired by the Christian idea of the trinity to which the Norse were exposed in later times).

The source of Odin's wisdom was the well of Mimir the Giant. Odin was said to have gambled one of his eyes with Mimir so he was often depicted as a one-eyed old man. Yet he was still generally depicted as strong, handsome, and warlike: armed with shield and spear. Odin has banquets to gods and heroes in Valhalla and Vingolf where he drank only wine. Other Gods and heroes were said to drink wine and other spirits as well as eat meat, but to Odin wine was his sustenance. When meat was placed before him, Odin gave it to his wolves Freki and Geri.

Odin was not alone in drinking from the well of Mimir. Mimir himself drank from this well with Gjallarhorn, the horn that Heimdall blows to announce the beginning of Ragnarök. Unfortunately for Mimir, he did not survive the Aesir-Vanir War fully intact. After a truce was declared, hostages were exchanged, but the Vanir believed that they had been cheated. The Vanir gave several great hostages to the Aesir and received in their stead Hoenir.

Hoenir was described as tall, handsome, and well-suited to be a chief. The Vanir were initially pleased with him because Hoenir gave good counsel, which he ultimately received from Mimir (drinking from his own well). But when Hoenir was at the Thing and did not have the counsel of Mimir, he was prone to not speak wisely but to allow others to decide. This made the Vanir grow displeased with him and so they captured Mimir and decapitated him in retaliation. Mimir's head was sent to Asgard where it was preserved in herbs by Odin. Odin spoke spells over the head, which allowed Mimir's head to engage in discourse with him, giving him good counsel and telling him secrets.

Thor and His Undead Goats

Thor guarded mankind from the wildness of nature, which was personified in the form of the Jotun. Thor held sway over the air and the temperature. As the deity responsible for rain and a good harvest, Thor was also a fertility god. Fertility Gods are not often thought of as male, and it is perhaps peculiarly Norse that they imagined God primarily responsible for their fertile harvests as being male. Thor was the principal deity immediately after Odin. He was Odin's son by Jord, one of Odin's wives.

Thor divided his presidency over nature with the Vanir although thunder and lightning belonged to Thor alone. Thor rode in a chariot drawn by two goats: Tanngnost and Tanngrisi. Thor had the ability to slay his goats and eat them, and then bring them back to life once more to drive his chariot. God was able to do this provided that he gathered up the bones of the goats and placed them in the hides. Like Loki, Thor had many epithets. Some of the better known of these were Einridi, Lorridi, Ving-Thor, and Riding Thor.

Chapter 2: Norse Gods and Goddesses

Few things reveal more about the climate of a people and a civilization than the Gods they worship. The people of the Norse world, commonly called Vikings in the English language, worshipped many gods. They were Gods of the sky, Gods of the weather, Gods of war, and Gods of the harvest. As we have already seen, Norse mythology also featured a legion of other colorful characters. These characters appeared in skaldic poems, sagas, and presumably in the earlier oral stories transmitted by the skalds and by others.

Indeed, the prominent presence of giants, ogres, goods elves and dark elves, dwarfs, dragons, and serpents is a characteristic that sets apart Norse mythology from some other popular mythologies that are studied today. Though it is certainly true that most mythologies feature monsters, beasts, and other embodied elements that the Gods and heroes must struggle against, in Norse myth these characters seem to take on a life and a significance somewhat different than in other mythical belief systems. Perhaps this is because the element of struggle in the life of Norse speakers was more present than in the lives of others. The people of the Norse world struggled against the elements. They struggled against their desires. They struggled against their enemies. They even fought amongst themselves endlessly.

But the purpose of this chapter is to examine more closely the Gods and Goddesses of the Norse pantheon. These Gods will be examined (as in other chapters of this book) in the form of the stories that were told about them by the traditional skalds and later by historians in the sagas. The examination of the Gods undertaken here will form a suitable preface to understanding the flavor of Norse mythology in contrast to the tone of other mythologies, like the Greco-Roman and Sumerian mythologies.

Theirs was a world colored by the blond-haired Thor with his mighty hammer Mjollnir. There, too, was Odin with his horse Sleipnir. There was the mysterious Frigg, the wife of Odin. And there was, of course, Loki who seemed as much unlike the Gods as he was kin to them. Interwoven with the tales of the Gods were the stories of the giants, set up as a foil that the Gods must always test their wits and prowess again. Chief among the various Gods and creatures of the Norse pantheon were the Aesir.

The Aesir and Vanir

We have already been introduced to Odin and Thor, the two chief gods in the Norse pantheon. They were ranked among the Aesir, the chief divinities of the Norse world. The *Poetic Edda*, *Prose Edda*, and other works about the Viking period and earlier tell endlessly of these Gods and their struggles. These Gods played prominent roles also in the lives and struggles of the heroes of the sagas, many of whom are thought to be actual historical figures.

As we have seen, the Vanir were Gods who existed in parallel with the Aesir. As the Aesir had their pantheon of Odin and twelve other chief Gods, the Vanir also had their pantheon, which included Freyja, her brother, Freyr, and their father, Njordr. The quarrel between the Aesir and the Vanir is referred to as the Aesir-Vanir War. The Vanir might be likened to the Titans of Greek myth, and like the Titans, they were generally regarded as great deities though somewhat lesser than the divinities that replaced them: the Aesir. The Vanir are sometimes grouped together as fertility Gods, representing a simpler way of life that preceded the warlike ways of the Vikings.

Before the Aesir-Vanir War, the Aesir Gods lived in peace and tranquility. It was a time before corruption, and events passed in Asgard in a goodly fashion. Things began to take a turn when three jotun maidens known as Thursar came into Valhalla. The entry of these giantesses caused enmity to grow between the Aesir and the Vanir. A woman called Gullveig was burned three times in Valhalla, and Odin threw his spear into the Vanir hordes to begin the war between the twain. The Vanir penetrated the walls of Asgard, forcing the Aesir to sue for peace.

A truce was called between the Aesir and the Vanir. This led to (as we have seen) an exchange of hostages between the two camps. The failure of this exchange is what eventually led to Mimir losing his head, which, of course, was necessary for Odin to acquire his famed wisdom. Though this loss of a head was an unfortunate event for Mimir, it did lead to Odin having access to all that he knew, a subject which we have already touched upon.

But the Vanir did not disappear completely. The more important of them entered the Aesir pantheon, in particular, Freyja and Freyr. Freyja was an important Goddess in Norse myth. Freyja follows men into battle and chooses from among the slain those that will accompany her in the afterlife. To her hall, fallen warriors would come, one of three places that people might go when they die. Freyja spends the rest of her time in mourning for her spouse, Odr, searching for him in distant lands. Freyja's brother is Freyr, perhaps the second most important among the Vanir.

Like Freyja, Freyr seems to hearken back to a pre-Norse time. His name occurs often in sagas and other surviving texts. He is responsible for the weather, fertility, and sexual pleasure. In some ways, Freyr seems to be the Vanir doppelganger to Thor. This dual and parallel nature to the Gods is unusual and does seem to suggest that the Aesir-Vanir conflict indicated a long-forgotten conflict between the Germano-Norse peoples and pre-Indo-European peoples (or another Indo-European group). Indeed, the presence of the Vanir (and even of the giants) suggests an earlier people that may have been replaced by the warlike Norse. Or, conversely, that earlier Norse Gods were replaced by Gods that originated from elsewhere.

The Treasures of the Gods

Loki was responsible for the great treasure that the Aesir acquired from the dwarfs. Loki cut off all the beautiful hair of Sif, wife of Thor, which caused great anger to rise in the God of thunder. Thor threatened to smash all of the bones in Loki's body, and this state of affairs was not remedied 'til Loki promised to fashion hair of gold for Sif that grew like true hair. For this, Loki had to turn to the dwarfs for help. Loki went specifically to the dark-elves, and these fashioned not only the golden hair for Sif, but a spear called Gungnir as well as a fast ship.

Loki wagered that the brother of a dwarf named Brokk, a certain Sindri, could not fashion treasures as grand as these that had been given to him by the dark-elves. The dwarfs fashioned three fine things in their forge: a ring called Drapnir, a fast-running boar called Gullinbusti who was able to run over the waters of the sea and through the air, and the mighty hammer Mjollnir. In the process of creating these, Sindri the dwarf was blinded.

These treasures were taken to Asgard where the Gods were to judge whether Loki's treasures were greater or whether the dwarfs had fashioned items dearer. Gungnir was given to Odin, who was well satisfied with the spear. The hair of gold was placed on the head of Sif where it immediately took root in the scalp. And Freyr was given the ship Skidbladnr, which was always blessed with good weather. It was then the turn for the dwarfs. They gave to the Gods their own three gifts of which the most remarkable was Mjollnir, which was given to Thor. The Gods judged that the dwarfs had won and that Loki would have to fulfill his promise and offer to the victors his head.

"Catch me if you can," said Loki, and he fled to a faraway land. The dwarf brothers Brokk and Sindri caught up with him. They asked for Thor's help in taking the head of Loki and the God of thunder agreed. Thor was about to remove Loki's head when the trickster God said that the wager did not call for his head and neck, but only his head. Brokk sewed Loki's lips shut and then tore out the instrument that he had used by reaching his fingers through the lips.

Loki and the Master Builder

Loki was numbered among the Aesir even though he was technically a giant. Among the Aesir, there was Odin in addition to Thor, Freyr, Njord, Balder, Tyr, Heimdal, Bragi, Hod, Vidar, Forseti, Ull, and Vali. Finally came Loki, who always kept secret commerce among the other giants and who would return to their ranks during Ragnarok. Loki was not related by blood to the other Aesir. He was the son of a giant called Farbati by a giantess called either Laufey or Nal. Loki and Odin became foster brothers and therefore was Loki counted among the Aesir even though he should more properly be styled as their nemesis.

As we shall see later, Loki was responsible for the death of Baldr. With a giantess called Angerboda, Loki fathered three children called Hel, Jormungand, and Fenrir. There is much to be said of Loki, and all of the important tales will be told of him in time.

Here we learn of Loki's role in the building of the world. In addition to his children by the giantess, Loki was also married to a woman called Sigyn who gave him several additional sons. Loki also became the father to the horse Sleipnir, which belonged to Odin.

After Midgard had been created, a giant offered to help the Aesir to build a large fortress as a protection against the jotun. In exchange, the giant, himself a jotunn, wanted the Goddess Freyja in addition to the sun and the moon. But the agreement stated that if the work was not completed by the first day of summer the giant, a master builder, would receive no wages. Loki urged the Aesir to make this agreement and the Gods were confident on their end.

But the giant was more adept than he must have appeared to the Aesir. With the help of his strong steed Svadilfari, boulders as large as mountain peaks were placed into formation. When there were three days remaining, only the castle gate needed completing, leading the Aesir to become ill at ease. It was unthinkable that they should have to surrender the Goddess Freyja, the sun, and the moon to the giant builder. The Aesir threatened Loki into helping them as they could not find any way out of their predicament.

Loki transformed himself into a beautiful horse, a mare, and ran past Svadilfari just as the steed was hauling stones into place. Of course, the horse took off after Loki (disguised as a mare). The master-builder followed the both of them, causing all work on the fortification to cease. This interruption led to the master-builder failing in his wager. The master-builder became angered, and he was slain with the hammer Mjollnir. Loki in the form of a mare sired Odin's horse Sleipnir, the fastest horse in the Norse world.

Freyja's Unusual Wedding

Thor nurtured a great hatred for the giants, and the theft of his hammer Mjollnir was the occasion for him to vent this hatred. Thor was incensed and he roped Loki into helping him discover the hammer's whereabouts. Loki discovered that Mjollnir had been taken by Thrym, who was the king of the giants. Specifically, Thrym was king of the race of giants or Jotun known as Rime-Thursar. Thrym said he would not return the hammer unless he could take Freyja as wife. It seems Freyja was quite popular as the most desired consort for overly ambitious giants.

Loki took the news to Freyja, who flatly refused to be the bride of the king of the Rime-Thursar. The Gods met in council and decided to use trickery to get around this particular predicament. They settled on dressing Thor in the clothing of a woman and sending him to Thrym as a bride. Of course, there was no intention for Thor to be anyone's bride. Once Thor made it into Jotunheim, where Thrym lived, he would retrieve Mjollnir and slay the king. Thor was accordingly dressed in the Necklace of the Brisings and other accouterments, and he was accompanied to his wedding by Loki disguised as his handmaiden. Thor even wore melodious jingling keys strung from his belt and was dressed in a matronly headscarf.

Thrym and his fellow giants gave the bride a royal welcome, commenting on her remarkable beauty. The giants even took note of the alacrity with which the bride drank her mead and ate her fare, taking enormous bites like a man. Mjollnir was brought in and the festivities were ordered to commence. At this juncture, Thor slew Thrym and his comrades. The God of thunder was able to take possession of his hammer once more.

The Norns

The Aesir and Vanir were not alone among the Gods in Norse mythology, although they were certainly the most important. There were also the Norns, great deities with supernatural powers. The Norns were Fates of a type, and there were very many of them. In spite of their number, three were regarded as being of paramount importance. We might think of them as first among equals in the Norns. These three were known as Verdandi, Urd, and Skuld, and they dwelled near the well that was known as Urd's Well.

This well was located beneath the great ash tree Yggdrasil. In this region, the Gods had their things, or assemblies, and the tree Yggdrasil dripped down dew. As has already been stated, the Norns were responsible for the destinies of men, a position of particular importance in the Norse world where men were very concerned with their honor, which was often shown by displays of courage in battle. The Norns were even responsible for the destinies of the Aesir themselves, rendering them old Gods of a type who were closely tied to the universe rather than connected with the creatures that had been formed within it.

The Norns were part of the indestructible laws of the universe, commuted in the form of the destinies of gods and men over which they presided. The Norns were present when children were born, determining then and there the fate of the child. There were Norns both good and bad. If a man outlived the time allotted for him as part of his destiny, it was the Norns who granted him permission to live on. Even though some Norns were dark, the orders of all Norns were regarded as equal and could not be overturned.

Chapter 3: The Children of the Gods

The Gods of the Norse pantheon were all related to each other by a complex network of relationships. This was just as true of the Norse Gods as it was of the Gods of other pantheons, such as the Olympian Gods of Greece and Rome, and the Gods of Egyptian myth. Many of the Gods were children of the Gods that had preceded them. The Gods, too, also fathered heroes by a number of women, including Goddesses, mortals, giantesses, and others.

Odin was the father of the Gods in more than just name. He was the elder of the Gods of the Aesir. He was also the true father of several Gods, including Thor and Baldr. Here we will explore some of the tales of the children of the Gods, learning how the lives of the Gods were just as craven and fraught with difficulty as the lives of the heroes and mortal men were. As we shall see, heroes like Sigurd engaged in acts that would be regarded as shameful today, and in many cases, the Gods themselves (as we have already seen) set a sinister example that these others followed.

Thor and Baldr

Thor and Baldr were sons of Odin by different wives. As we have seen, Odin had two wives who were called Frigg and Jord. Thor was the son of Odin by Jord while Baldr was his son by Frigg. Odin had other children besides, including Heimdal and Bragi. Odin was truly a progenitor of many groups among the Norse people. Indeed, Odin was regarded as the ancestor of several royal families, including the Volsungs, to which Sigurd belonged, as well the kings of Denmark through Odin's purported son Sigi. In spite of the numerous children of Odin, the importance of Thor and Baldr in Norse myth singles them out for special mention.

Thor was one of the chief Gods of the Aesir. He rode in a chariot that produced thunder and lived in a realm known as Thrudvang. In this place was a massive hall, which had 540 rooms. We have already seen that Thor was in possession of items of great worth, including the hammer Mjollnir. Thor was married to Sif, who was called "of the golden hair." This epithet was encapsulated in the myth regarding how Loki cut her hair and had to replace the original hair with hair of gold metal that was able to grow on its own. By Sif, Thor had children called Modi and Thrud. Thor also had a son called Magni by a giantess named Jamsaxa.

Baldr (or Balder) was a well-favored son of Odin. In Norse myth, Baldr was the God of piety and innocence. Light shone from his features his aspect was so bright. In character, he was kind, permissive, righteous, and wise. Baldr seems akin to Apollo in Greek and Roman myth, though the purity and innocence that he was associated with was rather distinct. Indeed, Baldr seems to be a God who the other Gods desired to shelter and protect. As the Gods were regarded as quarrelsome and sometimes prone to commit acts that would be regarded with horror in Christian times, Baldr stands out as a God apart.

Baldr lived in a fortified place called Breidablik whose name indicated that the place shone to such a degree that it could be seen from far and wide. In this place, no impure thought or deed could be committed or take hold. Baldr had children of his own. He was married to Nanna, who was the daughter of Nep. Forseti was his son. Baldr would be destroyed during the time of the twilight of the Gods, but he would return when the universe was reborn again. Baldr is regarded by some as a late addition to the Norse pantheon, his cult being mentioned in a work called *Fridthjof's saga*.

The Children of Loki

Loki formally belonged to the race of giants, as both of his parents belonged to this group, and he always maintained a secret loyalty to them. Loki himself was the son of the giant Farbauti and the Giantess Laufey, who was also known as Nal. He was counted among the Aesir because he became a foster brother to Odin, king of the Gods. Loki was not the only child of his parents. He had brothers called Byleist and Helbindi. As we have already seen, Loki was malicious by nature and he often got himself (and the other Aesir) into trouble. For example, when he cut off all of the hair of Sif, wife of Thor.

In Jotunheim, Loki father three children by a giantess. Her name was Angerboda and the three children that he sired were called Hel, Jormungand, and Fenrir. Fenrir was also known as Fenris Wolf, and he was a member of the race of wolves rather than a human. Fenrir was fierce and dangerous, much unlike the children of Gods like Odin and Thor. The other children of Loki did not fare much better. Jormungand was a serpent who was often referred to as the Midgard Serpent, while Hel was a vicious hag with half of her body a ghastly color. She was mistress of the domain of the dead and was confined to the depths far below Niflheim.

Jormungand was also relegated to depths far away from Asgard. He was tossed into the abyss of space, in which place he grew to an enormous size. The serpent grew to be so large that he came to be wrapped around the world. Indeed, Jormungand was long enough that, encircling the world, he was yet able to nip at his own tale with his fangs. The Midgard Serpent (the other name for Jormungand) therefore holds all the world encircled in his body.

The Fenris Wolf was reared in Asgard, though he was vicious and dangerous. Perhaps there was a special relationship between the Norse Gods and wolves like there was in Roman myth. In spite of the place of his nurturing, Fenrir grew to be ferocious and mean. The wolf was so fierce that Tyr alone had the wherewithal to bring him food. The food given him cause the Fenris Wolf to grow very quickly, and the Aesir resorted to binding him up. They tested the wolf's strength by binding him in a chain, which he broke. They bound him in a second chain, much stronger than the first, and he broke this one, too.

At this juncture, Odin sent Skrimir to the Dark Elves, who dwelt in the land of the dwarfs, supplicating them to create a chain that would be able to bind Fenrir. They created this chain from several strange things, including the beard of a woman, the sound of a cat's steps, a bear's sinews, the roots of a mountain, the spit from the mouth of birds, and fishes' breath. The chain they fashioned was called Gleipnir and it was soft to touch and thin rather than rough like a typical chain.

Fenrir was taken to an island and cajoled into placing the chain called Gleipnir around his body. The wolf knew that something was up so he agreed to this only if one of the Aesir would place their hand in his mouth. If the binds could not be broken, the Fenris Wolf would bite. All the Gods refused except for Tyr who placed his hand in the wolf's maw. Fenrir was bound, and he struggled to break free. The more he struggled, the tighter Gleipnir grew. As the Aesir would not free him, the Fenris Wolf bit off Tyr's hand. The Aesir took the chain and wolf and tossed these into a hole. This they covered with a boulder.

The wolf was more enraged than ever began to bite at everything around him until the Gods forced a sword into his mouth. This sword keeps the jaw of the wolf always parted so his howls can be heard by everyone. The Fenris Wolf is fated to remain like this until Ragnarok when he will be unleashed and rank among the fiercest enemies of the Aesir. These were not the only children of Loki. As has recounted elsewhere, Loki fathered sons by his wife Sigyn. He also was the father of Sleipnir, the horse of Odin All-Father.

The Domain of Hel

Hel, daughter of Loki, has been mentioned in passing before. She lived beneath the root of Yggdrasil, in Niflheim where it was cold, frightening, and dark. Hel was Loki's daughter by Angerboda. This Goddess (Hel, that is) had a singular appearance. It was said that one half of her body had a ghastly undead color while the other half had the appearance of human skin. She was covetous to obtain lives for her domain. She was also cruel and spiteful. The valleys surrounding her domain were known as the Hell-Ways. One had to cross a river called Gjoll to reach the domain of Hel. This river could be crossed through the use of a bridge known as the Bridge of Gjoll.

The Bridge of Gjoll was paved with gold, and the domain of Hel was spanned with lofty halls. As was typical with Norse legend, the accouterments of Hel's domain all had names. Her personal hall was known as Eljudnir. The knife that she carried was known as Famine while the dish that she ate from was called Hunger. She had thralls attendant upon her and these were called Ganglt and Ganglati. Even Hel's bed curtains had a name; these were called Glimmering Mischance.

It would not do for the warden of the Hell-Ways to be without a hound. Hel's hound dog was known as Garm, and he was bloody all over. This Goddess also possesses a rooster whose call is the harbinger of the universe's fall. Near the serpent Niddhog and the well of Vergelmir lies a place called the Strand of Corpses, or Nastrand. This was part of Hel's domain. Hel was also known as

Sister of the Fenris Wolf, a creature that, too, was the child of Loki who would be responsible for Ragnarok.

The Death of Baldr

As we have seen, Baldr, or Balder, was the God of purity and innocence. With the existence of Baldr, evil could never take a permanent foothold in Asgard or Midgard. Violence, of course, was a common part of Viking life, but violence would never gain the upper hand as long as Baldr lived. Over time, however, the Gods began to experience foreboding dreams that served as portents of disaster for both Gods and men. The Gods held a thing, or assembly, to investigate why they were having these dreams and what they might mean.

Odin decided to inquire of a long-dead seeress, or sibyl, what the dreams might mean. He rode his horse Sleipnir to Hel and compelled the sibyl woman to rise from her grave. The seeress asked who it was that had disturbed her repose. Odin gave the woman a false name, telling her he was the son of Valtam and his name was Vegtam. Vegtam, as he called himself, asked the woman whom among them was to die as the portents seemed to indicate. The woman said: "The mead for Baldr is prepared and the Aesir shall weep." Odin inquired whom it was that would bring destruction to the God Baldr, and the woman said that it would be Hod that would be the one responsible for Baldr's death.

Odin went on to inquire who it was that would avenge Baldr, and the seeress said that Vali, a son of Rind, or Rindr, would not rest until he had received vengeance for the death of the God of purity and innocence. The seeress rightly guessed that her inquisitor was Odin rathen than Vegtam. Odin had given several inadvertent clues that he was not a mortal, but a God in disguise. Odin replied that the woman was not a seeress, but an evil giantess and the mother of three thursar, or giants, who were the enemy of the Aesir. The woman was not perturbed, but told Odin to return to her when Loki was free and Ragnarok was drawing near.

Frigg, the wife of Odin, bound the Aesir and all things in the universe to oaths that they would do naught to harm Baldr. All in Valhalla felt secure in the belief that Baldr was safe. They felt so safe that they amused themselves by hurling objects at him as they were sure that no harm would come to Baldr. A woman came and asked Frigg, wife of Odin, what the Aesir were doing. Frigg said that they were hurling things at Baldr as they were sure that no harm would come to him as all had been bound by an oath. But Frigg admitted that only a small sprig of a plant called mistilteinn, or mistletoe, had not been bound because it was too young to swear to an oath.

The woman was really Loki in disguise, and he went away and took a branch of mistletoe. This God was up to mischief as usual. Of course, he was really a giant rather than a God, which explains a great deal. Loki carried this mistletoe to the place where all the

43

Gods were gathered. Loki found Hod and inquired of him why he was not hurling things at Baldr to amuse himself. Hod answered that he had no desire to harm Baldr and he had no weapon besides. Loki urged him to join in the games and gave him the mistletoe. Hod took the wand of mistletoe and launched it at Baldr, who fell down dead. This was the beginning of the end of the Gods.

The Gods were dumbstruck at what had happened. They were not permitted to seek revenge as they were in a sacred place. Odin above all understood how calamitous this deed of the death of Baldr was. It seemed that with the death of this God all the goodness in Asgard would flee, to say nothing of the goodness in the world. It would be Odin's wife Frigg who sent an emissary to Hel to learn what could be done to return Baldr to Asgard. Hermod, son of Odin, was the one tasked with going, and he took his father's horse Sleipnir on the journey, traveling as swiftly as he could.

The Aesir gave Baldr a great and solemn send-off. They took his body down to the ocean where a ship awaited. This ship was called Ringhorni, and it was pulled on land with the intention of being used as a burning pyre where it would be sent back to sea. But the ship was so large that it could not be moved from the land where it had been drawn up. The Aesir, therefore, sent for a giantess called Hyrrokin, bidding her to help. This giantess arrived on the scene riding a wolf that was pulled by serpents instead of by reins.

This Hyrrokin dismounted from her wolf. With ease, the giantess launched the ship from its place, while the Aesir utilized four beserker men to hold her wolf. The stays of the ship burst into flames, which angered Thor, but he was prevented from acting on his anger. The body of Baldr was placed on the ship, which caused Nanna great sorrow. The ship was lit with the assistance of Thor and Mjollnir. A dwarf happened to be in the wrong place at the wrong time, and Thor lit him up along with the ship. There were many in attendance at this event, including all the Aesir, the Valkyries, and others. Even Freyja came holding tight the reins of her cats and driving them. Even Cliff-Ettins and Rime-Thursar, jotun both, came to pay their respects.

Hermod went down to hell, which involved crossing the river Gjoll by way of the Bridge of Gjoll. On the far side of this golden bridge, Hermod met a maiden. He told her that he was in search of Baldr and asked her if she had seen him pass. She had seen him, and she told Hermod the route to hell so he could find Baldr. Hermod rode to the hall where Baldr was and found him. He asked Hel if he would be permitted to take Baldr with him, but Hel wanted to know how deep the affection for Baldr truly was. Hel said that if all things in the world would weep for Baldr she would let him go, but if one thing did not weep then he must stay.

Hermod returned to Asgard where he told the Aesir what Hel's requirement was. The Gods sent their messengers to request that all the things in the world weep for Baldr. These things did as they were asked. But the messengers were unable to obtain the agreement of Thokk, a giantess. Thokk said that Baldr had never brought her joy so Hel could keep him. Baldr therefore never left hell. It turned out that this character, too, was Loki in disguise.

Chapter 4: Heroes and Sagas

Saga is the term for the historic and legendary tales of Norse and Germanic history that appeared in the Middle Ages. The term saga literally means "something said," and many sagas dealt with historic events and kings. Today, many of the kings and histories mentioned in sagas are regarded as legendary. Indeed, in Sweden there is a list of kings whose only known record of having ruled comes from sagas; these kings are referred to as "mythical kings" or "saga kings" to indicate the lack of evidence that they existed.

Because saga referred to something said, they really represent the oral tradition of storytelling that was not only a part of Norse and Germanic life, but of early European life. Narrative storytellers (often referred to as bards in English) were common in many agrarian and pastoral societies in Europe. Indeed, such storytellers still existed in the Balkans in the 20th century, relying on stories that had been passed down for several hundreds of years rather than on written records. Research in this century found that these oral stories of battles and of people closely echoed the written histories that writers in countries like France and England had recorded hundreds of years, suggesting that this storytelling was an art and generally rather accurate.

Of course, this raises the question of whether the tales written in saga should be believed as representing real people and real historical events. The men that penned them beginning in the 13th century certainly the tales of the sagas were true, but it seems fair to admit that a little exaggeration may have happened along the way as stories were told and retold. So men described as giants or women described in various poetic ways indicating their beauty probably were not quite so grand as they were said to be.

What matters here is to try to understand what sagas meant to the speakers of Old Norse and Icelandic, and what role the heroes and other characters mentioned played in the daily lives of ordinary people of the times (in contrast to the "Vikings"). Again, we assume here that the sagas represent oral stories that would have been told in the Viking period, stretching from about the 9th century to the 12th century. This may seem a short period of time, but it was long enough for the Vikings to disrupt states in France and England, to establish new states in those areas and other places, and to colonize places as far off as the Faroe Islands, Iceland, and Greenland.

The heroes of the sagas were generally pagan, but were sometimes Christian. Naturally, in the context of this work (and this chapter), the reference of sagas will be directed toward mythical heroes and Gods from the pagan period. The line of distinction between the Christian and pagan world was not always a clear one. Indeed, as stated earlier, even the distinction between real events and fiction is not always clear.

Of course, it would be entertaining to presume that all one reads about mythical Gods and legendary heroes is fiction, but this is a presumption that cannot be made. Even the character of Sigurd (known as Siegfried in Germanic) from many Norse and Germanic legends, a hero who was said to have slain a dragon, is believed to have been based on a real king called Sigebert who lived in the Dark Ages. The grave of Siegfried was said to exist in Worms in Germany, but allegedly when the grave was unearthed it was found to be empty.

A sterling example of the blurred lines between real events and myths in the sagas is one of the most famous Icelandic sagas, the so-called *Egils Saga*. This saga tells the tale of a hero and poet called Egil who lived in the first generation of Icelanders. Much of the work, however, takes place outside of Iceland. Readers learn about Egil's forebears in Norway and about the reasons they left their homeland for Iceland. Although Egil is not universally regarded as a historical figure, some historians say this particular saga is the best example of a Scandinavian historical work about the 10th century, which presumes that the events of the story are actually true.

This again brings us to the question of the truth that underlies Norse mythology, even the stories about heroes. Indeed, this is a question that lies beneath the mythologies in many countries. There is always this question of whether this king or that was real, or whether Gods were originally men who lived and became Godlike because of their grandiose achievements. Could it be that all of the Gods of the Norse pantheon were real men, and that the only fictional elements, perhaps, were the supernatural ones like the composition of the universe, the various different worlds, and creatures like elves and dwarfs? In fact, we might even say that creatures like dwarfs, elves, or even the English brownie or Irish leprechaun may have been based on real characters or creatures.

But the intention here is not to stumble into a long discussion about whether the line between myths and histories is real. The real intention in this chapter is to state that this line is blurred (at least in the case of the Norse sagas), and to examine specific sagas because of their importance as canonical works in both Norse mythology and Scandinavian history.

Overview of Sagas

Egils Saga belongs to a type of saga known as Sagas of Icelanders. These are a specific category of sagas because they deal with the land of Iceland, which was believed to have been settled in about the 9th century. These sagas are also special because they are considered to have some value as works reflecting real history. *Egils saga* was written in Iceland in the 13th century by a man who is described as being a historian. This is important to note: although sagas may represent stories that were told orally, they were compiled by men who are usually described today as historians. This designation reflects both the fact that they often believed the stories that they told to have been true (presumably), and because many historians of today look to these works as sources of invaluable information about the time period in which they take place.

Egils saga is a little different from some of the other Sagas of Icelanders in that much of the action takes place outside of Iceland. *Egils saga* is regarded as historical in part because it refers to events that are known to have taken place, such as the efforts of King Haraldr to unite Norway, and how King Eirikr slew his two brothers. Some of the history cannot be verified, such as specific facts about Egill and his father Skalla-Grimr, although historians state that Icelanders at the time the Sagas of Icelanders were written regarded all of the contents of the sagas as fact. Again, they were believed to be based on transcriptions of three centuries' worth of oral tradition.

What is perhaps most interesting to the historian about sagas like *Egils saga* is the manner in which it has been transmitted to us today; that is, English speakers. *Egils saga* is told primarily in three different manuscripts, called W, M, and K (abbreviations of longer names). M, short for Mö›ruvallabók, is a collected work of the sagas of Icelanders, so it contains *Egils saga* in addition to others. Written in the 14th century, most modern translations derive from this work although they contain portions from the other two manuscripts.

W and K, also from the 14th century, are regarded as inferior in content to M. W is stored in a library in Germany while K exists in the form of two copies of the original manuscript from the 1600s. Although W and K are inferior, they contain portions of the story missing from the generally superior M, requiring the historian or other interested person to use all three to piece together the complete picture. Compiling the stories of heroes and mythological figures, therefore, requires more than simply consulting a single source, as is sometimes the case in other mythologies. In order to get the full flavor of Norse myth and history, one must consult many sagas and poems as this will allow you to complete the puzzle.

Heroes Mentioned in Sagas

The sagas are tales of gods, monsters, heroes, and historical figures. The dividing line between some of these groups is not always clear. Some of the more prominent characters in the sagas include Sigurd who is mentioned in the *Prose Edda*, *Poetic Edda*, the Nibelungenlied, and other works. There is also Thor, who takes the characteristic of both a hero and a God. Thor's place as a God recommends him to be treated in his own chapter rather than grouped together with the other heroes.

Among the most significant of the heroes was Sigurd, who we were briefly introduced to earlier in this work. Sigurd is a character of interest for several reasons. Sigurd, known as Siegfried in Germanic language works, is a character who seems characteristic of a particular culture. He is not like a Theseus of Aeneas: a founder of a state or civilization who seems almost idealized to suit the needs of the group for a heroic founder and legend. Sigurd comes across as a real man who has the failings of real men.

Sigurd and his exploits in Burgundy are the subject of numerous works from the period in which Norse and Germanic legends were transcribed, that is, the 12th to 14th century. This was a Christian period in which these pagan characters managed to retain some of their pre-Christian characteristics. So we learn about heroes like Sigurd coveting the wives of other men, or engaging in acts that would not have aligned with the Christian ideals that were becoming prevalent in the Norse world. Indeed, it is interesting that some of the Gods themselves, like Thor, more closely suit ideals of the Christian period than the heroes do, but that discussion is somewhat outside the scope of this work.

It is important to return to the geographic origin of many of the sagas. Most of the sagas left to us refer to the history of Iceland and Norway because the sagas of Iceland were preserved better than the corresponding tales of other places. These works were taken to Denmark in the 17th century and later and from there transmitted to us today. Therefore, many of the heroes in the sagas are characters who played a role in the history of Iceland and also Norway. Some of these characters are kings, and the sagas of this type are often classified as Kings' sagas.

There are many sagas of importance, both the Sagas of Icelanders and Kings' Sagas (as well as others). Many volumes can be written on the different sagas and how they should be classified or grouped. In this work, we mention the sagas so that the reader will understand how the knowledge of Norse mythology has been transmitted, and the problems that come from the blending of historical events with elements of fantasy. Some of the important sagas include *Grettis saga, Laxdaela saga, Njals saga, Egils saga (Egla), Arons saga Hjorleifssonar, Heimskringla, Hervarar saga, Sturlunga saga* and *Volsunga saga*. As an aside, works of the modern period bear similarities to the Old Norse idea of the saga. Indeed, J.R.R. Tolkien's Lord of the Rings has been translated in Icelandic as *Hringadrottins saga*, or Ring Lord's saga.

The Mead of Poets

Mead was the drink of common people in Norse times though it had a special association with poets and skalds. Odin was said to drink only wine, and only men that Odin favored could partake of this drink, which must have been very rare in the Norse world as the climate was generally too frigid for the vine to grow.

The story of the Mead of Poets involves a certain Kvasir, who was a traveler and teacher of men. Kvasir was invited to visit two dwarfs called Fjalar and Galar. They asked permission to converse with Kvasir and soon killed him, draining his blood into two crocks and then making it into mead in a kettle. Odin and the other Aesir were told the lie that Kvasir had drowned. Following this, the dwarfs received a visit from a giant called Gilling along with his wife. The dwarfs went to fish with Gilling. The dwarfs eventually reached land while the vessel of Gilling struck an obstacle and the giant was drowned. His wife, hearing this, began to lament loudly for a time, and the dwarfs tiring of this dropped a stone on her head, killing her.

When the son of Gilling and his wife, the giant Suttung, heard about the death of his mother, he went to Fjalar and Galar and marooned them on a tempestuous rock. Fretting over this, the dwarfs offered to Suttung the mead that they had made. Suttung accepted this and peace was reached between them. But Odin, learning of this, began to covet the mead. He tricked the thralls of Suttung's brother Baugi into slaying themselves and then (in disguise under the assumed name Bolverk) offered to do the work of nine men. Odin, as Bolverk, accomplished this and convinced Baugi to help him secure the mead of Suttung. Suttung refused to give Odin the mead and Odin used trickery to obtain it: disguising himself as a snake in addition to other things. Once he had the mead, Odin turned into an eagle and flew to Asgard, pursued by Suttung. Odin spewed forth the mead that he had obtained in Valhalla, which was given to practitioners of the art of poetry, while the mead dropped by Suttung in his pursuit was allocated for poetasters.

The Birth of Sigurd

There was a great king called Sigmund who was one of the ten sons of a king called Volsung by a Valkyrie named Ljod. We have spoken little of Valkyries but they were warrior handmaidens of the Gods, and they often played the role of messenger. Indeed, Ljod had come to Hunaland to bring an apple to a certain Reirir. After engaging in many adventures that were told in many Norse and Germanic tales, Sigmund would go on to father several sons, including Sinfjotli and Sigurd.

Late in his life, Sigmund paid court to a beautiful princess called Hjordis. This princess was the daughter of a king called Eylimi, and she was courted by several other prominent men. Eylimi gave his daughter Hjordis permission to choose her own husband and her choice fell on Sigmund even though he was now old. In spite of his age, the king was known for his prowess in war. Sigmund married Hjordis, which angered another king called Lyngvi, as he had also vied for her hand. When war became imminent, Sigmund transported Hjordis to a safe place and rode off into battle with his men. Sigmund fought valiantly until an old man joined the ranks of Lyngvi and brought low both Sigmund and Eylimi.

Yet Sigmund was still alive. Sigmund told Hjordis that he would certainly die and this fate could not be averted, but Hjordis should take the fragments of his sword and give them to the son she would have as she was then pregnant. This sword would be known as Gram and it would make their son among the mightiest of men in all the histories of the Norse people. Hjordis fled to the court of the king of Denmark disguised as he handmaiden. But the king noticed the great beauty of the lady and used clever questions to determine that she was the queen and not the servant. Though he had been deceived, the king offered to marry Hjordis after she gave birth and the lady agreed. She eventually gave birth to a son who would be known in Norse as Sigurd Fafnirsbane.

Regin and Sigurd

Sigurd was raised at the court of the king of Denmark, and he grew to be a man who was strong and above-average height. He also had the sharp eyes of his father Sigmund. Sigurd was placed into the care of a blacksmith named Regin who became his foster father. Regin was the son of a rich man and had two brothers. When his father, Reidmar, refused to give his two remaining sons his gold, one of the sons, Fafnir, slew him. Regin, deprived of his share of the patrimony, withdrew to the kingdom of King Hjalprek of Denmark, where he took up service as a blacksmith. Meanwhile, Fafnir transformed himself into the shape of a serpent and took all of his gold to a lair he made at a place called Gnita Heath.

Regin, who raised Sigurd, encouraged the young man to slay Fafnir and take the treasure. This would allow Sigurd to make a name for himself, an important thing for all young men of strength and prowess in the Norse world. Sigurd was assisted by his swift horse Grani, who was descended from Odin's horse Sleipnir. Sigurd's mother gave him the fragments of his father Sigmund's sword and these were shaped into a wondrous blade called Gram.

Before embarking on the odyssey to slay Fafnir, Sigurd decided firth to avenge the death of his father. He sought counsel from his uncle, the brother of his mother, Hjordis, and then he received men-in-arms from Hjalprek, the king of Denmark. Eventually, they found Lyngvi and made him their captive. They slew Lyngvi's brothers while Lyngvi himself was given the image of a blood eagle on his back. This is a nice way of saying that they carved lines in his back with a blade and pulled the lungs out.

The next thing to do was then to slay Fafnir, the brother of Regin in the shape of a great serpent. Regin suggested digging a trench and creeping to the lair at Gnita Heath in secret, while an old man suggested that several trenches be dug. One of these would be for Sigurd to hide in while the others would be canals for all the venom that Fafnir would certainly spew. Sigurd was concerned that Regin had not warned him to do this, and he began to suspect that his foster father had double-dealing in mind.

Sigurd unsheathed his sword and prepared to do battle with Fafnir. Fafnir moved so violently that tremors shook the earth. The venom from his fangs became rivulets that filled the canals. But Sigurd, who was hiding, managed to force his sword into the body of the serpent. Fafnir revealed that he was Regin's brother and asked the warrior his name. Sigurd considered telling a falsehood, but decided to tell the truth.

Because Fafnir was the brother of Regin, Sigurd owed Regin a wergild for the death of Fafnir. A wergild is a debt that is owed for the life of someone or when an injury has been done. Sigurd and Regin agreed that Sigurd would pay the heart of Fafnir to his foster father as wergild. Regin roasted the rest of the serpent and went to sleep. While Sigurd was preparing the heart, he burned himself on the hand and licked his fingers. He noticed that he could now hear the speech of some of the birds. Realizing that it was foolish to decline these powers for the payment of a wergild, Sigurd slew Regin and ate the heart himself. He now could hear the speech of all the birds, and they told him that he should travel to the top of a mountain and awaken a maiden who has been imprisoned.

Before this, Sigurd travel to Fafnir's lair where he acquired the serpent's gold as well as all of the treasure that he accumulated. This included a sword, a helmet, and other wondrous things. He tied these things to the back of his horse Grani, but the horse would not move until Sigurd was mounted upon the horse. Sigurd would go on to travel to Mount Hindarfjall where he encountered the shield-maiden, or Valkyrie, Sigrdrifa. He would go on to have other adventures until he was finally slain.

The Volsunga Saga and the Nibelungenlied

The *Volsunga saga* is one of the better-known Icelandic sagas. It is the tale of the Volsungs, the descendants of Volsung. Volsung was the ancestor of the important Nordic figure Sigurd. The tale of Sigurd's antecedents have already been told, specifically the events surrounding his birth to King Sigmund, and his rearing by his foster father, Regin. The Volsungs were regarded as an ill-fated clan, which made them a perfect subject in this, one of the more interesting of the sagas.

The Nibelungenlied also deals with the character of Sigurd, though he is called instead Siegfried. Interestingly, Sigurd and Siegfried do not have the same meaning in Old Norse and Old Germanic, respectively. Sigurd both have a portion of the term -sigi, which means "victory." In the Old Norse name, -urd is a variation of -ward, which means protection. In the Germanic version, -fried comes from -frith, which means "peace."

The Nibelungenlied, or the Song of the Nibelungs, is the tale of the death of Siegfried and its aftermath. Some of this saga has already been touched on, though some of the names and specifics may have slight differences in the Germanic story. The Nibelungenlied still placed Siegfried in Burgundy, but most forms state that he was raised by his father Siegmund at Xanten, now a small town in Germany. The Nibelungenlied deals with the marriage of Siegfried to Kriemhild in Burgundy, the rivalry between Kriemhild and Brunhild, and the death of Siegfried at the hands of Hagen, one of the vassals of the king of the Burgundians. Kriemhild later exacts her revenge, which results in the death of her second husband, the Burgundians that had accompanied her, the destruction of the kingdom of Kriemhild's husbands, and the demise of Kriemhild herself.

Chapter 5: Tales of Odin

As the king of the Gods and All-Father, Odin naturally appeared in many myths and tales. He was a fixture in the sagas, of which we know that at least some parts were regarded as historical. Odin, therefore, served in spirit as a motivator for this act or that, or justiciar in cases where justice needed to be dispensed or order maintained. Of course, Odin was not merely a supporting actor in myth. Odin was the center of his own myths. We have already learned how Odin gave his eye and gained wisdom through Mimir's head. In this chapter, we will learn how Odin served in the twin roles of host and guest.

Odin the Host and Odin the Guest

Odin was wise, and he liked to test his wits against others. He liked to challenge wise men by sending messengers offering these men the chance to test their wisdom against his. Although much maligned, many giants were renowned for their wisdom. There was a giant called Vafthrudnir who was famous for his historical knowledge, particularly regarding the history of the Gods and of the universe itself. Odin also found this area one of his own expertise, and he wished to try his brains against that of Vafthrudnir.

Frigg, the wife of Odin, did not believe this to be a wise course of action, and she urged Odin to try another flight of fancy instead. She knew that no one could match wits with this particular giant, and Odin was sure to lose. But Frigg's entreaties came to naught. Odin would not be dissuaded. All Frigg could do was hope that her husband's knowledge would be up to the challenge of testing wits against the giant. As usual with the Gods, Odin did not tell the giant his true name, but gave instead the name of Gagnrad. This name meant "the man who determines victory or luck."

Vafthrudnir agreed to test his wits against Odin, disguised as Gangrad, but only if the wager was that Odin would be trapped in the giant's hall if his knowledge was found wanting. The giant offered Gagnrad the seat for well-favored guests, but Odin declared that he was not equal to the honor of taking it. He said that it was his duty to speak from where he was and prove his worth. The giant was not perturbed by this, and he began to ask his guest questions about the universe, various geographic features in the parts of the universe where Gods dwell, and where the battles of Ragnarok are fated to take place, in addition to other things.

Gagnrad had no problem answering these questions. Indeed, he, in turn, asked Vafthrudnir his own barrage of questions. he wanted to know about how the world was made from the giant Ymir, about the differences between night and day, about where the giants had come from, about the god Njord, and about who would survive the onslaught of Ragnarok. He even wanted to know how the God Odin was fated to die.

There was no question among these that Vafthrudnir was unable to answer. Finally, Odin, as Gagnrad, had an idea. He asked the giant what the God Odin had whispered in the ear of Baldr, God of purity, when this latter God was laid on his funeral pyre and sent off in death. With this question, the giant Vafthrudnir realized that his guest was no other than Odin himself. Odin, therefore, retained his place as the wisest in the universe now that Mimir was dead.

Geirroed and Odin

Geirroed was the son of a king called Raudung. He was one of two sons; the other was called Agnar. Agnar and Geirroed as boys went fishing and spent the winter with peasants. The peasants adopted them, with the father adopting Geirroed. The peasants were actually Frigg and her husband Odin. Therefore it was Odin who adopted Geirroed. The peasant father, or Odin, told his foster son things in secret. Later, the boy tricked his brother onto a boat and pushed it into the ocean. He yelled that the trolls could have him. Geirroed then returned to his father's kingdom, where he became the king as his father had died.

Meanwhile, Agar had found his way to a giantess. Looking down from Asgard, Odin and Frigg saw that Frigg's foster son had fathered children with the giantess. In the meantime, Odin's foster son was ruling as a rich and well-favored king. Even worse, Geirroed was known widely for his stinginess. Odin refused to believe this so they sent Fulla, handmaiden of Frigg, to the court of Geirroed to determine if this was true. Fulla told Geirroed that he should capture a man whom the dogs of the kingdom would be afraid to bite. Such a man came to the kingdom, but it was really Odin in disguise.

The rumors about Geirroed were false, but Odin (in the guise of Grumbir) was tortured. Meanwhile, the son of Geirroed gave Odin a drink of mead, and the All-Father preceded to recite the names of the abodes of the thirteen Aesir, which were Vidi, Noatun, Glitnir, Folkvang, Breidablik, Thrynheim, the Mounts of Heaven, Soekkvabek, Valaskjalf, Ydalir, Thrudheim, Alfheim, and Gladsheim. Odin began to sing of other things pertaining only to the Gods. The man told Geirroed in honesty that he had forfeited the favor of Odin, which led the king to understand that Grimnir was Odin himself.

Geirroed, realizing that his guest was Odin, freed him from the trap that had been laid for him. In the commotion, Geirroed accidentally fell on the sword and died. His son, who was called Agnar the same as Geirroed's brother, became king in his stead. He ruled for many years as a good and wise king.

Chapter 6: Tales of Thor

Tales about Thor abounded. Thor was nearly as popular in the Viking period as he is today. As a God of war and justice, there would have been many temples and honored places devoted to Thor in the Norse world. Thor also would have been invoked in battle or before it as a way of assuring victory. Thor embodied many of the qualities that the Norse admired in men. He was physically strong, upright, handsome, and could be counted on to dispense justice fairly. it is sometimes puzzling that the Norse seemed rather obsessed with justice even though their Gods sometimes behaved unjustly. Even Thor himself was known to go into a rage and do things that would have been frowned upon or poorly understood in the Christian period. In spite of this, few Gods in the Norse period behaved with such uprightness as Thor.

Of course, most of the images that we have of Thor today come from sources long after the Viking period. Thor was a popular subject for artists in Scandinavian, German-speaking countries, and the British Isles from the 18th century onward. Because the sagas and other texts were preserved to a rather high degree in places like Iceland, and to a lesser extent Norway and Sweden, there was much information to draw on when piecing together the legends about Thor. Naturally, there has been much artistic license when it comes to depictions of Thor outside of canonical text, but the general message remains the same. Thor was one of the good guys, in contrast to a God-like Loki, whom we shall explore later. The message of Thor's goodness pervades many of the myths that we shall explore here.

Thor and Geirrod

Loki was often the source of troubles for Thor and the other gods. The tale of Geirrod and Thor is an example of Thor having to pick up the pieces from a mess that Loki created. Loki decides to dress himself as a bird, using a feather dress of Freyja's for this purpose. Dressed as a bird, Loki decides to listen in on the discourse in the hall of a certain Geirrod. Geirrod sees the fancifully disguised Loki perched on his window sill and he commands his men to capture the bird.

After Loki is captured by Geirrod, who is a jotunn or giant, he makes a deal with the giant to lure the God Thor into his home. Loki returns to Asgard where he tricks Thor into making the journey. Before they reach Geirrod's home, however, Thor is warned by a giantess named Grid that Loki is crafty and the God of thunder is walking into a trap. She gives Thor a magic belt in addition to other magical things.

After surviving near-drowning, Thor and Loki make it to the giant. Thor crushes two of the giant's daughters and agrees to engage in a game with Geirrod. The game is to toss a hot iron back and forth. Fortunately for Thor, he has a protective glove while Geirrod does not. This allows Thor to win the game. Thor hurls the iron through the chest of the giant, ending his life.

Thor's Journey to the Land of the Giants

Thor may have been a God associated with justice and righting a wrong, but he certainly was not peaceful. Indeed, wherever Thor went violence was sure to follow. Thor's mightiest challenge was to be opening a bag of food. Going on a journey with Loki and a servant, they came to Jotunheim, land of the giants. They came across the giant Skrymir who suggested that he travel with them and transport their things for them. While camping, however, Skrymir fell into slumber and Thor was unable to open the sack with their provisions.

Thor attempted to awaken the giant by hitting him upon the head with Mjollnir, his hammer. Each time, Skrymir thought that strikes were just the fall of an acorn and he returned to his slumber. The giants left the next day and the travelers soon reached an enormous fortification. Inside the hall of the fortification, they met the King of the Giants who challenged them to best him in feats. Each of the three had to prove that he was better at a particular skill.

Loki was to prove that he was the swiftest eater in the world. He went up against the king's servant. The competitors were set at opposite ends of a trough upon which there was placed massive quantities of food. Loki ate along the trough toward the center, but when he reached this place, he saw that his adversary had not only eaten the food and the bones, but the trough itself.

Thjalfi, the human, was next. He was a fast runner, swift enough to outrun any giant. The king called a giant who was able to swiftly outrace the human. The boy wanted a rematch and only narrowly missed winning. He tried even a third time, but the giant ran even faster. The King of the Giants had to admit that he had never seen a human run as fast as Thjalfi.

It was now the turn of Thor to prove that he could best his competitor. Thor's test was to drain cold mead from a mighty drinking horn in only two gulps. Thor drained as much as he could from the horn in three gulps, but this resulted in little change in the level of mead in the horn. Next, Thor was to test his strength. Thor merely needs to raise the cat of the King of the Giants from the ground. But the cat was Thor's height and very heavy. The cat arched its back every time Thor tried to lift resulting in Thor only being able to raise a single paw.

Thor flew into a rage and challenged any of the giants in a hall to a wrestling match. The king summoned his old wet nurse. The woman looked weak and old, but Thor was unable to outwrestle her. The three travelers prepared to leave the hall in defeat, but before that, the king revealed that all in the hall was an illusion. Loki lost his competition because his opponent was wildfire, which devours all. Thjalfi could not outwit his opponent because his opponent was thought itself, which can never be beaten by action. Thor could not defeat his opponent, which was old age, because age always catches up. The other competitions were illusions, too. The giant was so impressed by the performance of his guests that he swore never to allow them into his land again.

Hymir and Thor's Finishing Expedition

There were a number of lesser divinities who were neither Aesir, Vanir, nor giants. We have already been exposed to the Norns and the Valkyries, but there were also Gods who represented the forces of the natural world. There were several such deities of which some of the more important were Logi, whose name meant flame, Kari, whose name meant wind, Frosti whose name referred to the frost, Jokul whose name referred to the icicle, and so on. The most important of all was probably Aegir, also called Ler, who was a God of the sea.

One day, Thor and many of the other Aesir were gathered at a banquet given by Aegir. Thor intimated his belief that Aegir was not equal to the Gods of the Aesir, and Aegir in retaliation asked Thor to fetch a kettle large enough to brew mead for all of the Gods at once. This would by necessity be a very large kettle and all wondered how Thor would accomplish this. But Tyr came to the rescue. He told Thor that his grandfather, the giant Hymir, had such a kettle. His kettle was a mile deep, and it was impossible for anyone, god or mortal, to get a hold of it.

Thor and Tyr went to the land where Hymir lived, first stopping at the house of a certain Egil where they learned that the giant had gone out hunting. They then came across Hymir's wife who was a giantess with 900 heads. Tyr's mother was on the side of her son and Thor, and she hid them behind several large kettles. When Hymir came home, with icicles hanging from his beard, his daughter told him that he had visitors, and she named them as Thor and Tyr. Thor and Tyr emerged, and three oxen were prepared for their repast that night. Thor alone ate two of the oxen. The next day, Hymir suggested that they go hunting while Thor suggested fishing instead.

They rowed very far out to sea that day, giving the giant a fright. The giant began to fish for whales, pulling in two quickly. Thor used a bull's head as bait and tried to pull in the Midgard Serpent. The Midgard Serpent took the bait, and Thor struck him on the head with Mjollnir. But this was not enough, and the Serpent was able to slink back into the sea. When they reached home, Thor was able to draw the boat ashore and carry the whales without breaking a sweat. Hymir then wanted him to prove his strength by seeing if he could smash the beaker of Hymir into pieces. Thor hurled it against a pillar without success; then Tyr's mother suggested that he sent it against Hymir's head. Thor did this and the beaker split into pieces while Hymir's head remained as it was.

Hymir agreed to let Thor and Tyr have the mile-deep kettle for the Aesir's banquet if they were able to carry the kettle away from where it was. Tyr attempted this act first with no success. Then Thor tried. He was without success at first, but then he managed to toss the kettle so that it rest upon his head, carrying it that way. He began to leave the home of the giant, when Hymir sent an army of fierce giants and giantesses to follow him. Thor tossed the kettle to the ground and then used Mjollnir to slay the horde of giants and giantesses. Finally, Thor was able to make it back to the fete where the kettle was used to brew drink for the gathered Aesir.

Chapter 7: Tales of Loki

Loki was a well-known God in Norse times just as he is today. It seemed that the Aesir Gods were amused by him when they really should have been wary. The Norse myths and legends are rife with tales of Loki getting himself into this scrape or that, and of Loki needing aid in getting out of his assorted scrapes. Tales also abound of Loki getting others into scrapes and the Gods having to restrain themselves from their desires to do this or that to Loki out of anger.

Indeed, Loki is a character in a large number of tales. Perhaps Odin and Thor alone appear in more tales than Loki. Loki generally is a supporting character, serving the role as a foil to the wisdom of Odin or the relative goodness of Thor. One wonders if Loki really is the embodiment of the wicked or sinister side of man: a side that was just as important in the balance of life and death as the side that was concerned with innocence and justice. Here, two tales will be explored regarding the trickster God Loki. The first of these is the tale of the kidnapping of Idun.

The Kidnapping of Idun

Tales of Idun, or Idunn, are attested in several sources, most notably in the *Poetic Edda* and the *Prose Edda*. Idun was the wife of Bragi, and she was associated with youthful beauty and apples. The story of her abduction, or rape as it is sometimes called, involves Loki in a prominent place, getting into mischief as usual. The Gods would be very sore at the loss of Idun and, in typical fashion, they would threaten Loki into getting her back even though he was the one responsible for her "rape" in the first place.

The name Idun had several meanings. It might mean rejuvenator, the one who is forever young, or the one who rejuvenates. Her name here is Anglicized because the Norse character eth, or ð, does not exist in English. Really, her name should be Iðun or Iðunn. Throughout this book, we have generally used Anglicized versions of names in cases where the original letter does not exist in English.

The abduction of Idun occurred at the hands of the giant Thjazi. The story begins with Thjazi disguised as an eagle. After hitting this eagle with a poledark, Loki finds himself in the predicament of being attached to the bird. The eagle carries Loki further into the air as he flies. In consequence, Loki's feet are banged against all manner of things, like trees, rocks, and gravel stones. Loki soon begins to worry that his arms will be pulled out of their sockets. Loki and the eagle come to an agreement. The eagle will let Loki go if the trickster God promises to lure her out of Asgard.

Loki returns to Asgard where he finds Hoenir and Odin. Loki lures Idun to a forest at a time agreed upon by Loki and Thjazi. Loki gives Idun the lie that there were apples there that she would certainly desire to add to her collection. As Thjazi desired Idun to come to the appointed place with her famed apples, Loki tells Idun that she should bring her own apples from Asgard so she can compare those in the forest with those that she possesses. Idun travels to the place with her apples where she is snatched by Thjazi in the shape of an eagle. He flies away, taking the Goddess to Thrymheimr, his home.

With the loss of Idun, the Aesir begin to lose their youthful vigor. They have become old and frail. They gather at an assembly, or thing, where they attempt to discover where last the Goddess was seen. They realize that the Goddess was last seen with Loki, and they capture the trickster God and bring him to their thing. They threaten to beat Loki and torture him if he does not reveal what he knows about the disappearance of Idun. Loki says that he will bring Idun back if the Goddess Freyja agrees to allow him to use her shape of a falcon. This will allow God to search for the Goddess in Jotunheim, the home of the giants (of which Thjazi is one).

Freyja agrees to give Loki her falcon shape. Using this shape, Loki flies to Jotunheim, but finds that Thjazi is out fishing at sea. Idun is thus alone in the home of the giant. Loki uses his own powers to transform Idun into a nut. He places her in the grasp of his claws and flies off with her as swiftly as he can. Thjazi eventually returns home to find that Idun is gone. He turns back into an eagle and engages Loki in a chase. The falcon is able to fly into Asgard while the eagle catches on fire. The eagle falls at Asgard's gates. The Aesir slay the giant Thjazi, a death which, according to the Prose Edda, is greatly renowned.

The Last Day of Loki

Antecedent to Ragnarok, Thor and Loki had a quarrel. Thor left the hall of Asgard disguised as a fish. Loki hid in a waterfall called Franangrsfors, and it was in this place that we have apprehended by the Aesir. Loki was bounded up in the entrails of his own son, a certain Nari. Another son, Narfi, was transformed into a wolf. A snake full of venom was placed over Loki's face by Skadi. From this snake dripped poison. Loki's wife, Sigyn, had a basin that she used to catch the venom so it would not harm Loki, but when the basin became full, she had to leave for a moment to drain it. During this time, the venom fell upon Loki causing him to tremble and shake with such force that he created earthquakes.

According to another version of this story, Loki is put on trial because of his numerous crimes. In particular, Loki has attempted to murder Thor in the past, he was responsible for the death of Baldr, and various and sundry other things. A very large number of people have grievances against him. So says Forseti. No one is able to defend him, not even his wife Sigyn. As punishment, Loki's body is placed on top of three rocks, each representing a great crime that Loki has committed. Loki is bound with his son's entrails and a snake is wrapped around his face that drips venom.

We have already seen how Loki was responsible for the death of Baldr. This was the beginning of the end of the Gods. After the death of Baldr, there were three years of winter. As a result of this, the sun and moon (Sol and Munni or Sunna and Muni) are eaten by the wolves Skoll and Hati. The four dwarfs that hold up the sky drop it and as a result the stars fall from the heavens. Three cocks crow which results in the release of prisoners, which include the Fenris Wolf, Jormungand, and Loki.

Now free, Loki goes to Jotunheim, the land of the giants, where he boards the ship called Naglfar, which is waiting for him. This ship is made from the braided hair of the dead as well as their fingernails. Taking this ship, Loki goes to Asgard as captain among the giants.

Chapter 8: Lighter Tales of Norse Characters

Thor, Loki, and Odin may be fixtures in Norse tales, but there were those tales in which they were peripheral characters, or did not appear at all. Here, we will learn of some of the lighter or lesser tales of Norse legend, tales which still help us form an image of who the speakers of Old Norse were and what they believed.

The Marriage of Njord and Skadi

Njord, or Njordr, was one of those Gods whose domain was the weather. Njord was responsible for the direction of wind. This God also governed fire and seafaring. Men prayed to him when they wanted good luck on a voyage. He was also prayed to when men were at the hunt and desired good fortune there, too. Njord was originally of the Vanir living in Vanaheim. He was exchanged for Hoenir at the end of the Aesir-Vanir War, and from that time on he was numbered among the Aesir.

Njord dwelled in a place near the sea called Noatun. This place was known for the swans that abounded in the area. Njord was the father of Freyja and Freyr, who also followed him to the Aesir. The stepmother of the twain was Skadi, who was a giantess. Her father was the giant Thjazi whose death was brought about by the Aesir. Skadi went to Asgard to demand weregild for the death of her father and the Gods agreed to allow her to choose one among their number to be her husband. The catch was that she could not see the face of the man she chose, only the feet.

Skadi, the giantess, examined the feet of all the men that were then present in Asgard. In her mind, she had already decided that she wanted Baldr for a husband. The giantess came across a pair of feet that were strong and shapely. She knew that these belonged to Baldr and she happily chose these to spend the rest of her life with. As luck would have it, these feet did not belong to Baldr but to Njord. Skadi and Njord married, although they often quarreled. It seems that Skadi never got over her hankering for Baldr.

After the marriage, Skadi wanted to return to Thrymheim, where she was from, while Njord wanted to return to his own home of Noatun, where the swans and waterfowl flourished. They agreed to a schedule of twelve days, in which nine nights would be spent in Thrynheim and three nights would be spent in Noatun. Njord was not happy with the howling of the wolves and the other accouterments of the land of the giants, but Skadi herself disliked the screeching of the birds, which was very unpleasant to her ears. Eventually the twain went their separate ways. Skadi returned to her home of Thrymheim, where she became known as a Goddess associated with hunting and skiing.

The Apples of Immortality

The Gods of Asgard are not naturally immortal. It is the apples of the Goddess Idun who keep the Aesir in a state of youth. These apples of immortality can only be picked by the Goddess Idun. These apples grow east of Valhalla where lies a tree in a special garden. On one occasion, these apples were stolen. Loki was captured by a giant called Thjasse disguised as an eagle. This giant is also called Thjazi, and Loki's dealings with him would lead to the kidnapping of Idun (see the chapter on the tales of Loki).

The Story of Gerd and Freyr

Freyr, or Frey, was the son of Njord. He was very strong, brave, and handsome, even more so that his father. As one of the Vanir who came to the Aesir, he was another God associated with weather and fertility. He governed tillage. Men and women prayed to him for peace and prosperity. Under the special dominion of Freyr was the land of Alfheim and the good, or bright, elves.

Freyr was married to the daughter of a giant named Gymir. Her name was Gerd, and the story of their union is the subject of the present tale. One day, Freyr caught sight of Gerd while he was gazing at the wide world. He saw her strolling in her father's farm, and it seemed that she made the air and sea around her shine brighter. Freyr fell instantly in love, but he could not have her as she was a giantess. Out of his sadness, Freyr ceased eating and drinking. Njord was curious what was wrong so he sent Skirnir, a servant, to learn what was wrong. Freyr confessed that he was in love with Gerd and asked Skirnir to ask for her hand on his behalf.

Skirnir only agreed to go on this errand if Freyr lent him his sword, which could strike on its own when it wished to. Skirnir used trickery to convince Gerd to meet with Freyr. They agreed to meet after the passage of nine nights, nights spent in painful longing in Freyr's case. It was said that Freyr's love for Gerd was a punishment for the God sitting upon Odin's throne on one occasion.

Chapter 9: Ragnarok

The Gods were not above the power of those higher than them. They, too, must be subject to judgment. They too must perish when their allotted time has come. Ragnarok was the name of the Twilight of the Gods, the period when the end of the Gods draws near. The name Ragnarok can be taken to mean the Dissolution of the Gods or the Darkness of the Gods. The Gods knew that Ragnarok would eventually come. The coming of this time would be foreshadowed by evil portents, such as increased violence and ill behavior among men.

The Final Destiny of the Gods

Ragnarok will be heralded by the crowing of the Aesir cock in Vahalla as well as the crowing of Hel's cock in the Hell-Ways. Fjalar, the cock of the giants, also will crow, and hound of Hel will bay far down below Yggdrasil in Niflheim. The world will descend into wickedness for three years, and this will be followed by a long, snowy winter. No warmth will come from the sun, which will be swallowed by the wolf called Skoll. Another wolf will swallow the moon. The stars will be extinguished and earthquakes all around cause the world, even the mountains, to tremble. The Fenris Wolf and Loki both will be freed, and the Midgard Serpent will cause the waters of the sea to rear up and wash over the land.

Loki will steer a ship made up of the nails of dead men. Rime-Thursar and other giants will follow. All of these wicked creatures - Loki, the Fenris Wolf, the Midgard Serpent, the giant Rym, the Rime-Thursar - will be free to raise their hordes for battle. The Aesir also prepare for war with the sounding of the Gjallar-Horn. The Gods are roused, and Odin seeks guidance from Mimir's head. The two hosts meet on the field of Vigrid. Odin is first, dressed in his golden armor and brandishing Gungnir, his spear.

Odin and Thor, respectively, prepare to fight the Fenris Wolf and the Midgard Serpent. Thor fights Midgard Serpent and vanquished him, but only walks nine steps more until he falls down dead. The Fenris Wolf swallows Odin until God is vanquished. Other Gods among the Aesir die, too. Freyr is vanquished by Surty while Loki and Heimdal slay each other. Surt covers the world in flame and all things on the earth perish. This sets the stage for a new life. A new land rises, young and green. Plants grow without seed needing to be sewn. The sun and her daughter herald a new day. Those Aesir who did not die return, setting the stage for the All-Father, the governor of everything.

Chapter 10: Twenty Little Known Facts about Norse Mythology and Viking Beliefs

In this chapter, we provide a concise list of twenty facts that may help you develop a balanced picture of Norse mythology and the history of the period (and after).

Fact One: The Gods, Heroes, and Other Characters of Norse Myth and Legend Were Attested in Documents in the Old Norse Languages, the Progenitor of the Modern Languages of Scandinavia.

Norse myths have been better preserved than many other myths from peoples that lived in Europe between ancient times and the present. Remember that the Vikings lived in the Dark Ages. They were called "dark" for a reason. Education and learning had practically disappeared since the fall of the Roman Empire, and many peoples of Europe saw their societies turn retrograde compared to what had existed under Roman times. For this reason, we know little about many of the tribal peoples of Europe at this time because they left no records. We do however know a lot about the Norse and their myths. How can this be? Well, after the Norse were Christianized and began to be educated, they decided to record all the oral tales of their people and former

Gods in the sagas so that they would not be lost. These sagas can still be read today.

Fact Two: Most of the Old Norse Texts That Still Exist Today Come from Iceland.

Most of these sagas come from Iceland. This is because the Icelandic people were more diligent about preserving their records than the people in the other areas of the Norse world. Perhaps the reason is because Iceland had been settled so recently, only about two hundred years before the coming of the Christians, and the people wanted to remember how their ancestors had come to this land. Indeed, most of the people living at the time were descended from the original settlers, many of whom had specific mention in the saga. That is reason enough to preserve such valuable information, and so the Icelanders did.

Fact Three: Many Norse Legends Involve People Who Actually Lived and Were Not Merely the Stuff of Myth and Legend.

One thing that is learned from the Sagas of the Icelanders, like Egils saga, is that some of the events and people recounted are actually historical. This means that they were not made up or invented like the Gods presumably were, but they actually lived and breather just like you. This makes the dividing line between what is real and what is not in Norse legend difficult to measure sometimes. Surely certain things were false, but how can one tell if a particular human character was real or not? This interweaving of reality and fantasy is part of what makes Norse legend so interesting.

Fact Four: The Prose Edda and Poetic Edda Are Two Important Works from the Thirteenth Century That Serve as Invaluable Sources of Information About Norse Myth and the Time of the Vikings.

Eddas can be thought of as collections of tales, many of which are in poetic form. The Poetic Edda and Prose Edda are two important works that provide an invaluable resource about not only the Gods, but on how the Norse speakers viewed their world. How they related to it. Indeed, most people do not realize that most biographies of the Gods are pieced together from references throughout works like the Prose Edda and Poetic Edda, in addition to the various sagas and runestones from Scandinavia.

Fact Five: The Norse Personified Many Things in Their Cosmology as Gods or Humanlike Beings.

Another interesting thing about Norse myth and legend is that many things in their universe, like the Gods themselves, seemed to be the personification of this or that. At the center of the universe was the ash tree Yggdrasil around which moved nine worlds. In all of the realms that the Norse recognized, creatures like Gods, giants, dwarfs, elves, and other creatures all embodied things. This may be true of most mythologies, but the link between the idea and the personification of the idea is very clear in Norse myth.

Fact Six: The Norse Divided Their Gods into Two Main Groups: The Aesir and the Vanir.

The Aesir and Vanir comprised the two main groups of Gods. The Aesir were regarded as the chief gods in the Norse world. There were a total of thirteen Gods of the Aesir: Odin and twelve others. On the female side, Frigg presided over her own pantheon of Goddesses. The Aesir and Vanir fought in a conflict known as the Aesir-Vanir War. As a result of this war, there was an exchange of Gods and Goddesses between the two groups. Hoenir went to the Vanir. While Njord, Freyr, and Freyja went to the Aesir. They were permanently numbered as Gods of the Aesir from that point onward.

Fact Seven: The Norse Believed in Many Types of Beings Besides the Gods, Including the Giants, Elves, Dwarfs, Famous Horses, Monsters, and Others.

Norse myth has served as an inspiration to many people interested in fantasy for a number of reasons. The Gods are compelling as are there stories. This alone provides many with a source of inspiration. But one of the major things about Norse myth that inspires is its wide cast of characters, and most of these characters are not human beings. There are elves, dwarfs, giants, serpents, giant wolves, and many other things to provide fascination to those looking to be fascinated. The Norse invented fantasy, so if you are looking for ideas for your next story look no further than Norse legend.

Fact Eight: The Giants, or Jotunn, Were Particularly Important in Norse Mythology. They Even Sired Children by the Gods of the Aesir, Including Loki and Thor.

The giants were very important in Norse mythology. Although they were not as powerful as the Gods and lived in their own realms of Jotunheim or Thrymheim rather than Asgard, they were practically ubiquitous in Norse myth. Indeed, it is difficult to name an important Norse myth that does not involve at least one giant. They truly were the nemesis of the Aesir Gods although the Aesir really ought to thank them. If there were no giants, the Aesir would have likely died of boredom. There would have been no scrapes to get out of or problems to fix.

Fact Nine: According to Attestations from the Norse Period, the Giants Were Formed Before the Gods.

The formation of the universe and the creatures within it is one of the more interesting stories in Norse legend. The two main regions in the early days were cold Niflheim and not Muspellsheim. Heat from Muspellsheim melted ice from Niflheim, which eventually formed the giants. The Gods of the Aesir were formed later, after the cow Audhumla licked boulders of frozen salt.

Fact Ten: The Famous Trickster God Loki Was Actually a Giant, Though He Was Admitted into the Aesir Group of Gods.

Loki is one of the more interesting of the Gods in the Norse pantheon. Indeed, Loki is perhaps so interesting because he should not be there at all. Loki was, by birth, a giant. He was fathered by a giant and his mother was a giantess. Loki was only admitted into the Aesir because he was the foster brother of Odin. If it was not for Odin, Loki probably would have gotten his just desserts for constantly pulling Gods like Thor, Idun, and Baldr into scrapes. Loki would eventually return to the side of the giants during the cataclysm that formed the twilight of the Gods.

Fact Eleven: Thor Is Perhaps the Most Famous of the Norse Gods Because of His Mention in Media, Such as Film, Cartoons, and Comic Books.

Most people reading this work are familiar with Thor. Thor, the God of thunder, is easily the most famous character not only of the Norse gods, but of all of Norse myth. The image of a blond, helmeted God wielding a hammer symbolizes Norse myth more than any other. It is about as compelling an image as Hercules dressed in his bearskin or Perseus holding the head of the gorgon, Medusa. Thor forms part of the reason why people are so enthralled by Norse myth, even if modern retellings do not always align perfectly with the Thor that the speakers of Old Norse knew.

Fact Twelve: Although Attestations Are Not Particularly Clear on the Nine Worlds That Flank Yggdrasil, Today These Worlds Have Been Granted Specific Identities Based on Information from the Norse Period.

Although the Nine Worlds are generally not mentioned in sagas and skaldic poems from the Norse (Viking) period, modern scholars have created a list of what these worlds were based on information attained from texts, runes, and other sources. These words were:

- **Asgard:** Home of the Gods
- **Alfheim:** The land where the Godo elves lived.
- **Hell:** The home of the Goddess of the underworld. This land was also known by the Goddess's name, so "Hel."
- **Jotunheim:** Home of the giants
- **Midgard:** The middle world where most men lived
- **Nidavellir:** The land where the dwarfs lived

- **Niflheim:** An ice realm where the dead lived
- **Svartalfheim:** The land where the dark elves lived
- **Vanaheim:** The land where the Gods of fertility lived

Fact Thirteen: Odin Was the All-Father in Norse Myth: The Most Important Member of the Pantheon of Gods and Goddesses.

Odin was the equivalent in the Norse myth of Zeus in Greek mythology. Odin was not only the father of gods like Thor, he was also the symbolic father of Asgard. He was the father-figure who was important for keeping balance and justice in Asgard and the world below. For this reason, Odin was also known as All-Father. He features in many Norse myth, some of which detailing how he acquired his wisdom, or how he came about his horse Sleipnir.

Fact Fourteen: The Valkyries May Have Been Peripheral Figures in Most Norse Stories, but They Have Become One of the More Popular Subjects for Artists and Writers in the Modern Period.

The Valkyries are another enduring image of the Norse world. Part of this has to do with the ease with which the artist can create a powerful image of this character, while also the idea of warrior women is fascinating to some. Although sometimes described as Amazons, the Valkyrie were different from these characters of Greek myth. The Valkyries were not at war with men, but they were closely associated with them as well as with the Gods. The Valkyries chose among the fallen those who would be able to march in Valhalla after death.

Fact Fifteen: Norse Paganism or Odinism Has Experienced a Revival in Many Areas, Including Iceland.

Norse myth is becoming more popular today. And we are not just referring to reading about it and perhaps having the occasional dream or two. Norse paganism has been adopted by many as a religion, not unlike the religion that the ancestors of modern-day Scandinavian people would have practiced. This religion involves the worship of the Gods in religious ceremonies, and in specific beliefs about the afterlife and the relationship between Man and the Gods. What modern-day Norse pagans feel about elves, dwarfs, and monsters is anybody's guess. Norse paganism is said to be particularly popular in Iceland, where much of Norse legend and practices were preserved for hundreds of years.

Fact Sixteen: Frigg Was the Wife of Odin. She Was Believed to Know the Destiny of All Things, but Never Reveals Her Knowledge.

Frigg was a character who did not appear to often in Norse myth. Frigg was the wife of Odin, which meant that she served the role that Hera served for the Olympian Gods. But unlike Hera, Frigg was not known for her jealously. Indeed, it was said that Frigg played an important role in life. She was privy to the knowledge of the destiny of all living things. Though she has this knowledge, it is said that Frigg never reveals what she knows.

Fact Seventeen: The Dead Could Go to Several Different Places. They Could Go to the Domain of Hel, Beneath Niflheim. They Could Be Chosen by the Valkyries and taken to Valhalla. or They Could Be Selected by Freyja to Dwell with Her in Her Land of Folkvangr.

One of the aspects of Norse myth that always seems to fascinate people is what the Norse believed happened to people after they died. The Norse believed that many people who died, if not most of them, would go to the domain of Hel, far below Niflheim. Others would be chosen by the Valkyries to meet Odin in Valhalla. Yet others would be chosen by the Goddess Freyja to be welcomed to her hall in Folkvangr.

Fact Eighteen: Much of the Fame of Norse Myth Comes from the 19th Century When Works by Men like the Grimm Brothers and William Wagner Became Popular.

Much of our fascination with Norse myth today does not come from a permanent link with this past culture that has persisted to the present. Most of our modern-day information comes from sources that existed in the 19th century, when both literary works and artistic works about Norse myth became popular. This was part of the Romantic period, when men and women were beginning to rediscover various aspects of art and literature that had disappeared. This was also an age of nationalism, where Gods associated with Central Europe and Scandinavia began to take important roles as countries in these regions began to assert themselves internationally.

Fact Nineteen: Most Norse Myths Were Actually Written down in the Christian Period, After the Practice of Worshipping the Norse Gods Had Actually Disappeared.

People often forget that much of our knowledge about Norse myths comes from Christian historians who lived in Old Norse-speaking countries. Besides runestones, the Vikings left few records. The stories that had been told orally were occasionally recorded, but it was not until the written sagas began to appear that great works that could be preserved became "a thing." Christian historians are believed to have preserved these legends and myths because of what they represented in the culture of the people, rather than to preserve the memory of the worship of polytheistic gods. That being said, some figures from the Middle Ages responsible for the preservation of these myths and legends were known to be averse to speaking ill of the old Gods, even though these people had become Christians.

Fact Twenty: In English, Tuesday Is a Day of the Week That Originates from the Old Norse Language and Belief System.

Tuesday is an important day of the week. It comes after Monday and before Wednesday. Tuesday also is "Thor's day", that is, the day of the week associated with Thor. Although it may seem trite, the presence of this day in the English calendar reminds us that Norse's influence is not as great as Greek or Latin influence, but it is there.

Chapter 11: List of Norse Gods and Goddesses

The Norse pantheon was filled with gods, giants, good elves, dark elves, dwarfs, serpents, wise men, monsters of all sorts, and other creatures. Indeed, the wide variety of races and species in Norse myth and the fondness that the Norse and Germanic people had in naming these creatures appears to be a particular characteristic of the people and their religion.

In this chapter, we provide a list of the major figures in the Norse pantheon. Some of these characters are Aesir or Vanir, while others are giants and the like. These latter characters are generally only mentioned in the context of their association with the Gods. For example, giantesses who sired children with Gods are mentioned here. Another chapter could be written solely about giants, but that is outside the scope of this work.

[NOTE: All names in Old Norse unless otherwise indicated]

- **Baduhenna** (Germanic): A goddess attested in the annals of Tacitus. There was a grove in frisia dedicated to her.
- **Baldr**: A son of odin and brother to thor and vali.
- **Beyla**: One of the servants of freyr. She served alongside her husband, byggvir.

- **Bil**: Along with hjuki, bil is a child who follows the sun and moon in their path across the sky.
- **Bragi**: Norse god of poetry. He was the husband of idun.
- **Byggvir**: The husband of beyla and one of the servants of freyr.
- **Dellingr**: A god attested in the poetic edda and prose edda. He was the father of dagr, who was the personification of the day.
- **Eostre** (Old English): A Germanic goddess who gave her name to the festival of easter in some languages.
- **Forseti**: A Norse god of justice. He was the son of baldr and nanna.
- **Freyja**: Freyja was the twin sister of freyr and originally one of the vanir. She was associated with war, love, death, and was commonly featured in many poems and sagas.
- **Freyr**: Originally one of the vanir, this god was the son of the god Njordr as well as the twin brother of Freyja. He was a fertility god with phallic associations. He was associated with the royal house of Sweden and was sometimes known as Yngvi-Freyja.
- **Frigg**: One of the goddesses of the Aesir, and the wife of Odin.
- **Fulla**: A Norse goddess and an attendant to Frigg, wife of Odin.

- **Gefjun**: A goddess associated with ploughing, the harvest, and certain parts of the world, including the island of Zealand in Denmark.
- **Gersemi**: The sister of Hnoss and the daughter of Freyr.
- **Gerdr**: A giantess, or jotunn, who was the wife of Freyr.
- **Gná**: A goddess who serves as a messenger and errand woman for Frigg, the wife of odin.
- **Gullveig**: A goddess who was burned three times by the Aesir and three times reborn. Some have argued that she is the same as Freyja.
- **Hariasa**: A goddess attested in a single artifact from Germany. She may have been a war goddess.
- **Heimdallr**: A god associated with knowledge. He was also said to be the source of social classes in the human race. This god had many other names. He possessed the horn Gjallarhorn and the horse Gulltopr.
- **Hel**: Daughter of odin and ruler of the underworld.
- **Hermod** (Old English): A son of the god Odin, Hermod (or Hermodr) is sometimes referred to as a messenger god. His name means the spirit of war.
- **Hjuk**i: Along with bil, hjuki is a child who follows the sun and moon in their path across the sky.
- **Hlin**: This goddess appears in the *poetic edda* and is associated with Frigg, wife of Odin.
- **Hnoss**: The daughter of freyr and the sister of Gersemi. Her name means "treasure."

- **Hodr**: A blind god, he was a son of Odin and Frigg. He is also called Hod. He is tricked by Loki in being involved in the death of baldr.
- **Hoenir**: Originally one of the Aesir, Hoenir is sent to the vanir as part of the exchange that ended the Aesir-Vanir war.
- **Hretha** (Old English): Also known as Rheda, this goddess is mentioned in Anglo-saxon works where she gives her name to a month.
- **Idun**: A goddess associated with youth and apples. She is the wife of Bragi.
- **Ilmr**: A goddess attested in ancient skaldic literature.
- **Yngvi**: Yngvi was the progenitor of a line of kings in Norway Yngvi is sometimes associated with freyr.
- **Irpa**: A goddess attested in Icelandic sagas and other literature. She is prayed to as a goddess of victory.
- **Jord**: One of the wives of odin.
- **Lodurr**: A god infrequently mentioned in the sagas, Lodurr was said to have a role in animating the first human beings, Askr and Embla.
- **Lofn**: A gentle goddess associated with the arrangement of marriages.
- **Loki**: A trickster god and one of the Aesir. He was frequently in collusion with the giants and would become one of their leaders during Ragnarok.

- **Modi and Magni**: Sons of Thor, their names mean courage and strength.

- **Mani**: The male personification of the moon in Norse myth.

- **Meili**: A son of odin and a brother of thor.

- **Mimir**: A god of wisdom, Mimir loses his head in the aftermath of the Aesir-vanir war, but the head is preserved by odin in order to draw from his wisdom.

- **Nanna**: Daughter of nep and the wife of baldr.

- **Nerthus** (Germanic): A German fertility goddess attested as early as the roman imperial period.

- **Njord** (Old English): A god of the Vanir, Njord (or njordr) is associated with the sea, ships, seafaring, and wealth. He is the father of Freyja and Freyr by his sister who is not named in the sources.

- **Njorun**: A goddess attested in sagas whose role is not entirely clear. She may be associated with the earth.

- **Odr**: A god whose name means "the frenzied one."

- **Odin**: The king of the gods, he is the leader of the Aesir. He is married to Frigg, and is the father of thor, baldr, as well as others.

- **Rán**: A Norse goddess who personified the sea.

- **Rindr**: Alternatively, rind, she was a giantess who was the mother of vali.

- **Sága**: A goddess associated with wisdom. She is specifically tied to Sokkvabekkr.

- **Sandraudiga** (Germanic): A goddess attested in a single inscription from the low countries.
- **Saxnot**: Or Seaxneat, a god attested in the genealogies of the kings of Essex, and the eponymous god of the Saxons, a German tribe.
- **Sif**: Sif, of the golden hair, wife of Thor. Mother of Modi and Thrud.
- **Sigyn**: The wife of Loki and a goddess of the Norse pantheon.
- **Sinthgunt** (Old High German): The sister of the embodied sun, she is attested in a sole Germanic work.
- **Sjofn**: A goddess of love.
- **Skadi**: A jotunn, or giant, associated with hunting with bows, mountains, skiing, and winter.
- **Snotra**: A goddess of wisdom attested in the *prose edda*.
- **Sól**: Also known as Sunna, this goddess was associated with the sun.
- **Sunna**: Another name for Sól (see above).
- **Syn**: A goddess associated with refusal undertaken in defense. She was mentioned in the poetry of the skalds as well as the *prose edda*.
- **Tamfana** (Germanic): A Germanic goddess who had a temple attested in the roman period by Tacitus.
- **Thor**: One of the more well-known among the Norse gods, thor was the son of odin and the god of thunder. He

was also a fertility god. Thor was frequently mentioned in sagas and poems.

- **Thorgerdr Holgabrudr**: The sister of Irpa, this goddess is attested in Eddas and sagas.
- **Thrud:** Daughter of Sif and Thor.
- **Tuisto** (Proto-Germanic): The god who was the ancestor of the Germanic peoples.
- **Tyr**: A god whose name is attested in many runestones.
- **Ullr**: The personification of glory in Norse belief.
- **Vali**: A son of odin by rind.
- **Vár**: A goddess associated with bonds and oaths.
- **Vór**: Another name for Vár (see above).
- **Vidarr**: A son of odin by the giantess grid.
- **Ve**: A brother of odin and one of the earliest among the Aesir. His father was born.
- **Vili**: Another brother of odin and one of the earliest of the Aesir. He was a son of born, like Odin.
- **Zisa**: A Germanic goddess attested in late manuscripts from the region around Augsburg.

Frequently Asked Questions

1. What geographic region does the term Norse mythology refer to?

Norse mythology refers to the mythology of the speakers of Old Norse, the people who are commonly referred to in English as Vikings. Although there is some discrepancy between the term we refer today as Viking and what people in the Viking age though, it can be said that the "Vikings" – coming from the several nations of Scandinavia – would have been a representation of the people who spoke this language and followed this mythology. Old Norse is a Germanic language and the myths of Norse legend are generally regarded as overlapping somewhat with Germanic myths.

But the reality is a little more complex. Most of Norse mythology that we know of today comes from texts that originate from Iceland and Norway. Therefore, the Norse mythology that we know may be regarded as reflecting more accurately these areas rather than the other areas where Viking people lived. So some historians would argue that the legends of the Danes and Swedes may have been slightly different from some of the information that we have about Norse myth from the sagas and poetic texts. The beliefs of the German tribes to the south of

Scandinavia were likely even more divergent although there would have been some commonalities.

2. When did the period of Norse mythology and beliefs end?

The period in which the Norse mythology and belief system came to an end would have spanned from the 11th century to the 12th century. This the period when the regions where the Vikings hailed from became Christianized, a slow process which likely took a century or more. Iceland and Norway were the first areas of Norse settlement to be Christianized. Denmark followed perhaps three decades after Norway while Sweden was the last, this country not being Christianized until the year 1150.

But even with Christianization, some remnants of the antecedent culture remained. Indeed, a famous Norwegian skald told his king that he would not speak ill of the old Gods nor would he decline to mention them in his works. Indeed, all of the sagas and other poetic works from which most of the contents of this book on mythology ultimately derive were written in the Christian period even if they were based on earlier oral traditions. For several reasons, Scandinavia and related regions like Iceland retained aspects of their pagan heritage longer than other areas that had been Christianized. This allowed the myths to be preserved to a greater extent than other pre-Christian European mythologies.

Also, there was a fervent interest in Norway and Iceland in particular in holding on to tradition. Beginning in the 17th and 18th centuries, mythologies began to be compiled based on earlier works like the Sagas of Iceland and the Prose and Poetic Eddas. Even today there is a desire to retain or even salvage aspects of a belief system long-since vanished.

3. What are some of the names of Odin?

Odin was the supreme, father deity in Norse mythology. Odin was akin to Zeus in Greek myth or Jupiter in Roman myth. As epithets are very common in certain mythologies (including Norse myth), Odin had many names. Besides the name of All-Father, as Odin was often called, this supreme deity was also known as:

- **Valfather:** Father of the Slain
- **Gaut or Geat:** The Creator
- **Bolverk:** The Worker of Misfortune
- **Baleyg:** The One with Flaming Eyes
- **Sigfather:** The Father of Victory
- **Ygg:** The Awful (also may indicate a yew tree)
- **Har:** The High One
- **Herjan:** God of battles
- **Gagnrad:** The Determiner of Victories

- **Jafnhar:** Even as High
- **Thridi:** Third (a name-bearing similarity to the Christian idea of the trinity)

4. Were there important distinctions among the Gods?

Just as in Greek mythology, the Gods were divided into groups, although in the Norse case these groups did not actually represent a difference in age. This is in contrast to Greek myth in which the Titans were the elder Gods that were overthrown by the Olympians. The first great characters in Norse myth were the giants, who were mostly slain by the Aesir: the chief group of Gods. But the giants were not completely slain. One would remain, and this giant would procreate, which would set the stage for Ragnarok.

The Aesir consisted of Odin and twelve other Gods. Besides Odin, these Gods were Thor, Freyr, Njord, Balder, Tyr, Heimdal, Bragi, Hod, Vidar, Forseti, Ull, and Vali. Another important group of Gods were the Vanir. They were rivals to the Aesir, with many of the Vanir occupying positions similar or even identical to those of the Aesir. For example, Thor, one of the Aesir, comes across as being rather similar to Freyr, one of the Vanir. The Aesir and the Vanir eventually went to war with one another, which resulted in an exchange of hostages by way of truce. It was in this fashion that Freyr and Freyja, who became important among the Aesir, entered Asgard from their original home.

In addition to the Aesir and the Vanir, there was another important group known as the Norns...

5. So... who were the Norns?

The Aesir and Vanir were not alone among the Gods, although they were certainly of central importance. There were among them also the Norns, great Goddesses with supernatural abilities. The Norns resembled the Fates, and they were large in number. In spite of their numbers, three among the Norns were regarded as being of paramount importance. We might think of them as first among equals in the Norns. These three were known as Verdandi, Urd, and Skuld. They dwelled near the well that was known as Urd's Well.

6. Who were the Valkyries?

The Valkyries were female warriors closely related to the Norns. Their role was tied to the fates of warriors and men, as the Norns were. They specifically had jurisdiction over death in battle and success in war. Famously, the Valkyries were delegated by Odin the task of choosing those who are fated to be slain in battle. They are referred to also as shield maidens or the Maidens of Odin. As depicted in art from much later than the Norse mythological period, they were very beautiful. They were often depicted with blond hair that was separated into two long braids.

The Valkyries made their home in Valhalla where they served as the Aesir's cupbearers. There was a division among the Valkyries. One half of them were the celestial Valkyries. These were the original maidens. The other half of them were halfbreeds: they were half human and half celestial. This later class had originally lived among men and only later took up residence with the Gods. The number of celestial Valkyries is sometimes given as nine times nine. The most well-known of these were Geir-Skogul and Gondul.

7. Is Norse mythology all fiction or is some of it based on historical events?

It is not always easy teasing apart reality from fantasy in the context of Norse tales. Norse mythology has been left to us in the form of poems and sagas that were written in the early Christian period of Scandinavia; that is, between the 12th century and 14th century. Some of these records were remarkably well preserved, especially in the case of the sagas dealing with Norway and Iceland. This is because the Icelanders preserved much of their records from the Middle Ages over the centuries, and much of these records had to do with Iceland and with Norway, where most Icelanders had presumably come from.

The issue is that the historians of the Middle Ages were not only interested in preserving the pre-Christian knowledge, but they also perceived some of the events that had been related to be historical rather than mere myth. This is not difficult to understand, as Iceland was an area of recent historical settlement and some of the heroes associated with the settlement of Iceland were historical people who would have had living descendants rather than merely names from the distant past.

The long and short of it is that Norse mythology has been transmitted to us in the present in the form of poems and sagas, and some of these records clearly refer to historical figures. Of course, tales about historical heroes are sometimes intertwined with stories about the Gods, dwarfs, and other figures who are not considered historical. Therefore, the dividing line between reality and fantasy is sometimes clear although it is not always.

8. How does one tell reality from fantasy in the sagas?

Some of the figures of Norse sagas are known to be historic. Figures like kings and other leaders are likely to be attested in multiple places, which makes it easier for historians and scholars to determine if they were real people or just fantasy. We have spoken in the past of the mythological kings of Sweden. They are considered mythical because they are attested only in sagas, poems, or runestones, and therefore cannot be verified from sources that are known to be objective.

For example, the rulers and leaders of other European states are commonly attested in multiple sources. They may be attested in records from France, Italy, and England, confirming that these were most likely people that truly lived rather than the inventions of writers. When a figure is only mentioned in one source, and there is no physical proof that the person lived, this makes it more difficult to confirm the existence of said person.

This is particularly a problem in Scandinavia where many of the buildings and other monuments were built of wood until fairly recently. This means that any physical record that might be construed that a person actually existed was not likely to survive the centuries as such monuments would have in other places. Think about Ancient Egypt. We can say that this Pharoah or that actually lived because they are not only attested in the literature, but have monuments like pyramids, tombs, and obelisks that confirm their existence and give a rough estimate of when they lived.

9. Is Norse mythology related to other mythologies?

The question of the relationship that Norse myth has with other mythologies is an interesting one. Norse mythology has some features that render it distinct from other mythologies. The Valkyries, elves, dwarfs, and other non-human creatures give Norse myth a fantasy quality that is quite divergent from Greek or Roman myth, for example. It is fascinating to ponder the reasons why Norse myth moved in this sort of direction while the Greco-Roman myth went in another.

But in spite of these singularities, there are some aspects of Norse myth that seem to harken back to a very early Indo-European source of Norse myth. Ragnarok was the twilight of the Gods, the period when the Gods, giants, and most creatures in the world would be destroyed. But they would be recreated anew when the world would be reborn. The world would be repopulated from just two people. This sort of history does not have a precedent in other well-known European mythologies. This story does suggest South Asian ideas of destruction and rebirth, particularly the story where Brahma destroys the world and recreates it again. Perhaps some other elements of Norse myth can be tied to a South Asian or Near Eastern, i.e. Proto-Indo-European, origin.

10. Who were the Vikings and what role did they play in the propagation of Norse myths or beliefs?

The Vikings were warriors who left their homeland in the Scandinavian countries to pillage and settle in foreign lands. The Vikings who went West primarily were Danes and Norsemen who came from modern-day Denmark and

Norway. The Vikings who went to the East are less well-known because recordkeeping in this area was not as strong, with the exception of the Byzantine Romans in the far south. The Vikings who went East were primarily Swedes and Geats (or Goths) who came from modern-day Sweden.

Although it might be supposed that the terrors that the Vikings caused allowed Norse myth to be remembered, the myths and legends of the Norse primarily are due to the records that were kept primarily in Iceland. It is true that the historians of the 18th and 19th century who sought to rediscover the Vikings were able to turn to these sources to learn more about the people who conquered and enslaved them. To say that they were fascinated by these myths is an understatement.

11. What was the Nibelungenlied, and is this work considered part of the Norse canon?

The Nibelungenlied is a work that originates from the German world, although the character that it centers on was a figure in Norse myth, as well. Of course, the dividing line between Norse myth and German myth is somewhat of an invisible one as the Norse were a Germanic one. Because of relative isolation, the Norse people developed a mythology that diverged from Germanic myth. It is also true that there would have been some local Gods that would never have been universal. So while Thor and Odin may have had places in both Scandinavia and the German lands, other deities like Badhudenna would have remained in their local areas.

Although the Nibelungenlied is not generally regarded as canonical in Norse myth because it is a Germanic work that focuses on a Germanic historical figure, Siegfried, or Sigurd, was also an important figure in Norse myth. He is attested in works from Iceland in addition to the Nibelungenlied (which, by the way, is the saga of the ring of the Nibelungs). There are some similarities in the stories, although there are occasional differences in the names. Even the names Siegfried and Sigurd have different meanings in their respective languages.

Fact Twenty: In English, Tuesday Is a Day of the Week That Originates from the Old Norse Language and Belief System. Although the Old Norse language is a Germanic language, the names of heroes or even Gods occasionally are named differently in the Norse and more southerly German worlds. Part of this has to do with the nature of Norse practices in which many figures had various epithets and many names. We have already examined the many names of Odin, but even lesser figures often had more than one name.

Although the languages of Old Norse and Old Germanic, or Proto-Germanic, would have had some level of similarity, much like Spanish and Italian, or Spanish and

Portuguese, this did not mean that alternative names always had the same meaning. For example, Sigurd in Old Norse does not have the same meaning as the name Siegfried in the Germanic language, even though the -sig or -sieg portion referred to the same Germanic word.

12. Why does Norse mythology have such an appeal in the modern world of today?

The Enlightenment period in European history occurred in the 18th century. This movement, which was also known as the Age of Reason, began in France sometime earlier and really became a continental movement that spread to other countries in the 18th century. During this period, European philosophers and artists underwent somewhat of a Renaissance in which they began to reexamine their social organization, religion, and wider belief system. Specifically, philosophers began to question that a religious approach to life really met all of the humanistic needs of educated men living in a changing world.

This sort of paradigm shift in the way people viewed their world made Norse myth appealing. The Norse beliefs were a Northern European mythology and belief system that were very divergent from Christianity. Also, Norse beliefs gave people from Scandinavia and Germany a culture that they could turn to as nationalism and a sense of ethnicity became more important in Europe. The Romantic period in the 18th century was really a continuation of the ideals of the Age of Reason, but played out in a more artistic way. Because Norse beliefs seemed so different from Christianity, it appealed to those who were looking for alternatives to what must have been somewhat of an overbearing cultural construct.

13. Was Loki counted among the primary Norse Gods or Aesir? Is it fair to say that modern works seem to suggest that he was an enemy of the Gods?

Loki was ranked among the twelve Gods of the Aesir, even though he technically was a giant. Both of Loki's parents were giants, or jotun, but Loki was brought up as the foster brother of Odin. Loki was accepted by the Aesir as one of their own, even though they often quarreled with him or were displeased with him. They even imprisoned him on occasion.

Modern works seem to accept Loki as more of an evil character, even though his position in Norse myth was somewhat equivocal. Loki certainly was not perceived as good, but the Aesir did not generally question their loyalty to him. Because good and evil are more rigidly defined in Christian thinking, it makes sense that Loki is regarded as evil as his behavior would suggest this label. Through an examination of the Norse Gods reveals that they all did evil things, even Thor. Thus, the modern construct of Loki as an enemy of the Gods is an oversimplification that comes from a time in which people view the world, life, and human nature differently.

14. Did J.R.R. Tolkien draw inspiration for his works from Norse myth?

Norse and Germanic myth are regarded as very important sources of inspiration for the works of John Ronald Ruel Tolkien. Tolkien would have read some of these myths when he was a child. The images he gained from what he read must have been accentuated by the strange environment of the Cape (now South Africa) where he spent some of his formative years. Tolkien went on to study languages at university, where he eventually went on to teach.

The aspects of Tokien's works that clearly draw from Norse and other Germanic myths include the subject and plotline of his most famous work, the Lord of the Rings. This work was inspired to some degree by the Nibelungenlied, which was the tale of the Ring of the Nibelungs. Other aspects of Tolkien's works that draw from Norse and Germanic legend are the presence of elves, dwarfs, and dragons. These supernatural creatures seem commonplace in fantasy today, but their construct in the Western world clearly stems from Norse and German legend.

15. Were the Gods of Norse myth fundamentally different from the Gods in other mythologies?

Many peoples saw their Gods as being people not unlike themselves. This was especially true of the Greeks, who saw the Olympians as quarreling amongst themselves like humans, but it is also true of the Norse. The Norse Gods, even when they are specifically identified as being just, good, and the like, clearly engage in acts that are very human. They lie and trick each other. They murder people (sometimes innocent) in a rage.

This humanness of the Norse Gods, therefore, makes Norse mythology somewhat similar to some other mythologies, especially Greco-Roman. The Greco-Roman belief system generally saw their Gods as being part of families that were not unlike the human family. There are some mythologies where the Gods are thought of as being much better than humans, like the Egyptians, for example, but the Norse religion, in this regard, is not singular. The Norse Gods give the impression of being very, very human.

16. **Why did the people of Iceland and other areas preserve the myths and tales of their sagas even though their societies had changed in the Middle Ages?**

The preservation of sagas and other records in places like Iceland probably represented a desire to preserve historical and cultural traditions in the face of a rapidly changing culture. In places like England and Germany, the old beliefs were swept away so thoroughly that they were practically forgotten. This is not true in Iceland where many of the sagas and poems were about real people who settled the island of Iceland during the historical period. In preserving these stories of heroes they also preserved the legend and tenor of the Gods, who were closely associated with the heroes whether in embodied form or as inspiration.

17. **Who was Hel? What was the Norse concept of Hell?**

The Norse believed that Hell was the domain of a Goddess known as Hel. Hel was Loki's daughter by a certain Angerboda. This Goddess had a singular appearance. It was said that one half of her body had a ghastly undead color while the other half had the appearance of human skin. She was covetous to obtain lives for her domain. She was also cruel and spiteful. The valleys surrounding her domain was known as the Hell-Ways. One had to cross a river called Gjoll to reach the domain of Hel. This river could be crossed through the use of a bridge known as the Bridge of Gjoll.

The Bridge of Gjoll was paved with gold, and the domain of Hel was spanned with lofty halls. As was typical with Norse legend, the accouterments of Hel's domain all had names. Her personal hall was known as Eljudnir. The knife that she carried was known as Famine while the dish that she ate from was called Hunger. She had thralls attendant upon her and these were called Ganglt and Ganglati. Even Hel's bed curtains have a name; these were called Glimmering Mischance.

18. How accurate is the portrayal of the Gods and Goddesses in media today, such as film and print media?

The portrayal of Norse Gods today has been colored by the religious climate in which we live in today. it is easy for people to forget or ignore the extent to which society in the West has been shaped by Christianity. Characters like Thor, Odin, and the other Gods are generally sanitized somewhat in order to keep with the impression that they are "good" or "just." On the other hand, characters like Loki may be exaggerated in the other way to make them seem "worse" or "evil" in keeping with the strictly dichotomous construct of good and evil in Christian thinking.

19. Why has Norse mythology become popular outside the Norse and Germanic world?

To answer this question, all one really has to do is think about why Norse myth was popular in the Romantic period. People in this time were disillusioned to some degree with their own world, and harkening back to a different type where people lived and thought differently from the present allowed them to escape. There was sort of a fantastic sentimentality there, and this is obvious in some of the art from the period. The Gods are presented as good-looking and larger than life, with long blond braids and tall helmets. The reality that the Viking period was a time of extreme brutality where people were enslaved, slaughtered en masse, buried alive, and the like is often forgotten. People still use mythology and fantasy as a form of escape today.

Conclusion

The mystique that Norse mythology possesses shows no signs of going away. Perhaps it might be better to refer to it as fascination, but the appeal of Norse myth and legend does owe something to the clear distinction that exists between their world and ours. The Norse world was one where Gods were practically as cruel and mischievous as the men and women they ruled. They named all their lands, but could not prevent these lands from being destroyed by giant, serpent, and wolf.

This, too, is what draws so many to the world of Norse myth. This was a world filled with a wide cast of characters. It was a world in which the Gods were perhaps less interesting than the forces that they struggled against. The Greeks told tales about men battling monsters, and Gods siring offspring with mortal women. But the Norse tales often involve God and giant or God and serpent with no human presence at all.

The world of Norse myth was a treasure trove for the imaginative mind. It was a world of jotun and Rime-Thursar, of good elves and dark elves, of dwarfs and Valkyries. Indeed, human beings seem to be observers in this world of the Gods rather than central characters. Perhaps it is this which makes Norse mythology so interesting. The stories were not so much about human characters as they were about the embodied things of the universe: things taking the shapes of Gods, giants, elves, serpents, wolves, and dwarfs.

Today, we relegate most of the Norse world of myth and legend to fantasy, but to the Norse speakers, it was all very real. Some of these people became Vikings: people who left their homeland to pillage, enslave, and engage in nearly as much mischief as their Gods did. And lest one believe that only the trickster God Loki got up to evil deeds and thoughts, one need only read this tome again to jog one's memory. Even Gods like Odin and Thor were often possessed of the urge to kill this thing or that merely because they were angered or annoyed.

The Viking world was in many ways an extension of this belief system. Perhaps this is the reason why you are reading this work. Your goal may be to take a journey into the mind of a Viking warrior or maiden; to understand how they lived and why they lived in the manner that they did. It really is not very hard to understand them. One need only look at the example set by their Gods to understand that quarrelsomeness and often violent temper were regarded as just as much a part of normal being as purity, innocence, and the sorts of things that other religions make idols of.

It seemed the Norse truly recognized that Man was possessed of a dual nature. If one element of this dual nature superseded the other, then the whole would come crumbling down. The Norse world existed in a measure of balance between the good things and the bad things. The bad things - like the evil creatures of the

Norse world - generally outnumbered the good ones, but as the good element was generally embodied in the form of powerful Gods, the balance was always maintained.

The Norse mythological cycle presents a sort of history. As this history moved forward, as the Gods and heroes accumulated more and more tales of their exploits, the world became old. Eventually, Baldr died, and all the purity and innocence that was part of the delicate balance of life vanished. This was the beginning of the end of the Norse Gods. Perhaps this was what Ragnarok truly signified: a world that had grown so old that all the innocence was gone. A world that becomes like this was headed for destruction: destruction headed by the bad elements like the giants, wolves, serpents, and the God/giant Loki.

In the first chapter, we were introduced to the formative stories of the Norse myth. Not to say that these tales were the earliest, but they dealt with the earliest times. We learned about the great tree Yggdrasil and the Nine Worlds it surrounded. We learned about the fire of Muspellsheim and the ice of Niflheim. From the ice of Nifleheim came the first Gods. Before them were the giants. Both groups nurtured by the great cow Audhumla. We learned about Asgard, home of the Gods, and Jotunheim, home of the giants.

It was next the turn of the Gods to take their rightful place on center stage. The main body of Norse Gods were known as the Aesir. Odin was the lead, and he was joined by twelve of other Gods, including Thor and Loki. Formally, Loki was a giant, but he had been adopted by Odin so he was numbered among the gods. There was also Odin's wife, Frigg, who led her own cohort of Goddesses. Besides these, there were the Vanir, some of whom were accepted into the Aesir after the Aesir-Vanir War. There were also other important divinities like the Norns. Of course, there were also those beautiful shieldmaidens: the Valkyries.

The Gods sired many children, as they do in all mythologies. They were divinities - sort of the alpha males and females of the universe - so it was somewhat natural that they would be fruitful and multiply. Interestingly enough, the tendency for Gods like Odin, Thor, and Loki to have many children did not rope them into trouble as it did Zeus, who had jealous Hera to worry about. In the third chapter, we heard tales about the children of the Gods. If these tales seemed to be an extension of the tales of the Gods themselves, they were.

The Gods were the fixtures of Norse myth, but they were joined by the heroes of legend. Gods like Thor almost took the form of heroes, but in the fourth chapter, we discussed men like Sigurd and his father Sigmund. These men belonged to the unfortunate race of men called the Volsungs, men whose lives were recounted in the tale called the Volsunga saga. Of course, there was much more to be said about Sigurd, also known as Siegfried. He slew Fafnir and so was sometimes known as Sigurd Fafnirsbane. The tale of Sigurd (or Siegfried) was told in many places. Once we gained an understanding of the nature of the sagas, and how the

Sagas of Icelanders were somewhat different, we examined two particular tales: the *Volsunga saga* and the *Nibelungenlied*.

Next, it was the turn for particular Gods and Goddesses to take center stage. Just as the Greeks had their tales of Zeus, Heracles, Hephaestus, and Artemis, so, too, did the Norse have their tales of Odin, Thor, Prometheus, and Freyja. All of these tales were discussed as part of the attempt to construct the natural world that the Norse lived in. Our natural world may be one of science and reason, but the natural world of the Norse was once inhabited by gods, giants, and other often mysterious creatures.

Then came time for the twilight of the Gods: Ragnarok. This is a subject that always looms over a discourse in Norse mythology. Ragnarok is that thing that one has a prescient feeling about. One knows it is coming and before one realizes what has happened, the Aesir and Jotun have gone to war and the universe has been turned to dust. But that destruction is nothing more than an opportunity to create the world anew. The speakers of the Old Norse language knew that there was always a tomorrow. There would always be Gods looming large in their lives. There would always be giants lurking under the hills over yonder. This was the world the speakers of this language inhabited, and it is reborn every time someone takes the step of learning about these people and their Gods.

Made in the USA
Coppell, TX
17 December 2019